THE COMPLETE REFERENCE TO
ANGELS IN
THE KORAN (QUR'AN)

THE COMPLETE REFERENCE TO
ANGELS IN
THE KORAN (QUR'AN)

Kermie Wohlenhaus, Ph.D.
The Koran translated by John Medows Rodwell
Annotation by Kermie Wohlenhaus, Ph.D.

KERMIE & THE ANGELS PRESS   TUCSON, ARIZONA

To contact the author or order
additional copies of this book
Kermie & The Angels Press
P. O. Box 64282
Tucson, AZ 85728
www.KermieandtheAngels.com
KermieandtheAngels@gmail.com

This edition was prepared for publication by
Ghost River Images
5350 East Fourth Street
Tucson, Arizona 85711
www.ghostriverimages.com

Cover design by Kermie Wohlenhaus

ISBN: 978-0-9832300-9-0
Library of Congress Control Number: 2014914853

Printed in the United States of America
First Printing: September, 2014
10 9 8 7 6 5 4 3 2 1

Dedicated to the Divine and the Glorious Angels

Table of Contents

13

MICHAEL

ANGELS HARUT AND MARUT

MESSENGERS

Introduction

The Koran (Qur'an) is the sacred text of Islam which Muslims believe to be the revelation of God or Allah. "Koran" or "Qur'an" literally means "recitation." This sacred text was given to Muhammad from God by the angel Gabriel (Jubril). The revelations and recitation continued over 23 years. It began in December 22, 609 AD, when Muhammad was in his 40's and was completed in 632 AD, the year Muhammad died. Angels play an important role throughout the inspired scriptures of this sacred text. Islamic religion and culture has a rich and deep angelic tradition.

There are over 109 verses regarding angels in *The Koran (Qur'an)*. *The Complete Reference to Angels in The Koran (Qur'an)* is a compilation of angelic verses in their entirety. Angels are mentioned by name in *The Koran (Qur'an)* and are also known by their duties in fulfilling Divine Will. For simplicity, this reference is broken into categories starting with Angels, Gabriel, Gabriel as Spirit, Michael, the Angels Harmut and Marut, followed by Messengers. Angel references or implied references are underlined for easy identification within the text. This is an important foundation text for further study into the role of angels within Islamic teachings.

The Complete Reference to Angels in the Koran (Qur'an) is one of a series of books compiled into a volume called *The Complete Reference to Angels in Sacred Texts*. This series also includes *The Complete Reference to Angels in the Bible, The Complete Reference to Angels in the Book of Mormon,* and *The Complete Reference to Angels in Other Sacred Texts*. This series is a foundation text for the field of Angelology, the study of angels.

The English translation used in this text is by John M. Rodwell. As with all translations, there is modern criticism, but it is considered a viable translation and has lasted the test of time.

May Allah and the angels bless you in your journey through this sacred text.

Kermie Wohlenhaus, Ph.D.
www.KermieandtheAngels.com

ANGELS

Sura 2 Al-Baquarah (The Cow)

Sura 2:28-31 - Lord speaks to the angels and is informed of their names by Adam

2:28 When thy Lord said to the <u>angels</u>, "Verily, I am about to place one in my stead on earth," they said, "Wilt thou place there one who will do ill therein and shed blood, when we celebrate thy praise and extol thy holiness?" God said, "Verily, I know what you know not."

2:29 And he taught Adam the names of all things, and then set them before the <u>angels</u>, and said, "Tell me the names of these, if you are endued with wisdom."

2:30 They said, "Praise be to Thee! We have no knowledge but what Thou hast given us to know. Thou! Thou art the Knowing, the Wise!

2:31 He said, "O Adam, inform them of their names." And when he had informed them of their names, He said, "Did I not say to you that I know the hidden things of the Heavens and of the Earth, and that I know what you bring to light, and what you hide?"

Sura 2:32-40 - When angels told to bow down and worship Adam, all worshipped, save Eblis

2:32 And when we said to the <u>angels</u>, "Bow down and worship Adam," then worshipped they all, save Eblis. He refused and swelled with pride, and became one of the unbelievers.

2:33 And we said, "O Adam! dwell thou and thy wife in the Garden, and eat you plentifully there from wherever you list; but to this tree come not nigh, lest you become of the transgressors."

2:34 But Satan made them slip from it, and caused their banishment from the place in which they were. And we said, "Get you down, the one of you an enemy to the other: and there shall be for you in the earth a dwelling-place, and a provision for a time."

2:35 And words of prayer learned Adam from his Lord: and God turned to him; for He loveth to turn, the Merciful.

2:36 We said, "Get you down from it, all together: and if Guidance shall come to you from me, whoso shall follow my guidance, on them shall come no fear, neither shall they be grieved:

2:37 But they who shall not believe, and treat our signs as falsehoods, these shall be inmates of the fires; in it shall they remain for ever."

2:38 O children of Israel! remember my favour wherewith I shewed favour upon you, and be true to your covenant with me; I will be true to my covenant with you; me therefore, revere me! and believe in what I have sent down confirming your Scriptures, and be not the first to disbelieve it, neither for a mean price barter my signs: me therefore, fear you me!

2:39 And clothe not the truth with falsehood, and hide not the truth when you know it:

2:40 And observe prayer and pay the legal impost, and bow down with those who bow.

Sura 2:90-94 - Whoso is the enemy of Gabriel, Michael and the angels is an enemy of God

2:90 And thou wilt surely find them of all men most covetous of life, beyond even the polytheists. To be kept alive a thousand years might one of them desire: but that he may be preserved alive, shall no one reprieve himself from the punishment! And God seeth what they do.

2:91 Say: Whoso is the enemy of <u>Gabriel</u> – For he it is who by God's leave hath caused the Koran to descend on thy heart, the confirmation of previous revelations, and guidance, and good tidings to the faithful –

2:92 Whoso is an enemy to God or his <u>angels</u>, or to <u>Gabriel</u>, or to <u>Michael</u>, shall have God as his enemy: for verily God is an enemy to the Infidels.

2:93 Moreover, clear signs have we sent down to thee, and one will disbelieve them but the perverse.

2:94 Oft as they have formed an engagement with thee, will some of them set it aside? But most of them believe not.

Sura 2:95-101 - When the apostle from God affirmed revelations to them, they threw the Book of God and followed sorcery as taught by two Angels, Harut and Marut at Babel

2:95 And when there came to them an apostle from God, affirming the previous revelations made to them, some of those to whom the

2:96 Scriptures were given, threw the Book of God behind their backs as if they knew it not:

2:97 And they followed what the Satans read in the reign of Solomon: not that Solomon was unbelieving, but the Satans were unbelieving.

2:98 Sorcery did they teach to men, and what had been revealed to the two <u>angels</u>, Harut and Marut, at Babel. Yet no man did these two teach until they had said "We are only a temptation. Be not then an unbeliever." From these two did men learn how to cause divisions between man and wife: but unless by leave of God, no man did they harm thereby. They learned, indeed, what would harm and not profit them; and yet they knew that he who bought that art should have no part in the life to come! And vile the price for which they have sold themselves, – if they had but known it!

2:99 But had they believed and feared God, better surely would have been the reward from God, – if they had but known it!

2:100 O you who believe! say not to our apostle, "Raina" (Look at us); but say, "Ondhorna" (Regard us). And attend to this; for, the Infidels shall suffer a grievous chastisement.

2:101 The unbelievers among the people of the Book, and among the dilators, desire not that any good should be sent down to you from your Lord: but God will shew His special mercy to whom He will, for He is of great bounty.

Sura 2:154-158 - Infidels shall be the milestone of God, angels and of all men

2:154 They who conceal aught that we have sent down, either of clear proof or of guidance, after what we have so clearly shewn to men in the Book, God shall curse them, and they who curse shall curse them.

2:155 But as for those who turn to me, and amend and make known the truth, even unto them will I turn me, for I am He who Turneth, the Merciful.

2:156 Verily, they who are infidels and die infidels – these! upon them shall be the malison of God and of <u>angels</u> and of all men:

2:157 Under it shall they remain for ever: their torment shall not be lightened, and God will not even look upon them!

2:158 Your God is one God: there is no God but He, the Compassionate, the Merciful.

Sura 2:170-173 - He is pious who believeth in the angels

2:170 These are they who have bartered guidance for error, and pardon for torment; But how great their endurance in fire!

2:172 This shall be their doom, because God had sent down "the Book" with the very truth. And verily they who dispute about that Book are in a far-gone severance from it.

2:173 There is no piety in turning your faces toward the east or the west, but he is pious who believeth in God, and the last day, and the underlinedangels, and the Scriptures, and the prophets; who for the love of God disburseth his wealth to his kindred, and to the orphans, and the needy, and the wayfarer, and those who ask, and for ransoming; who observeth prayer, and payeth the legal alms, and who is of those who are faithful to their engagements when they have engaged in them, and patient under ills and hardships, and in time of trouble: these are they who are just, and these are they who fear the Lord.

Sura 2:200-206 - God should come down to them overshadowed with clouds, and the angels, and their doom shall be sealed

2:200 A man there is who surpriseth thee by his discourse concerning this life present. He taketh God to witness what is in his heart; yet is he the most zealous in opposing thee:

2:201 And when he turneth his back on thee, he runneth through the land to enact disorders therein, and layeth waste the fields and flocks: but God loveth not the disorder.

2:202 And when it is said to him, "Fear God," the pride of sin seizeth him: but he shall have his fill of Hell; and right wretched the couch!

2:203 A man, too, there is who selleth his very self out of desire to please God: and God is good to his servants.

2:204 O believers! enter completely into the true religion, and follow not the steps of Satan, for he is your declared enemy.

2:205 But if you lapse after that our clear signs have come to you, know that God is Mighty, Wise.

2:206 What can such expect but that God should come down to them overshadowed with clouds, and the angels also, and their doom be sealed? And to God shall all things return.

Sura 2:245-249 - Angels shall bear the Ark

2:245 Fight for the cause of God; and know that God is He who Heareth, Knoweth.

2:246 Who is he that will lend to God a goodly loan? He will double it to him again and again: God is close, but open handed also: and to Him shall you return.

2:247 Hast thou not considered the assembly of the children of Israel after the death of Moses, when they said to a prophet of theirs, "Set up for us a king; we will do battle for the cause of God?" He said, "May it not be that if to fight were ordained you, you would not fight?" They said, "And why should we not fight in the cause of God, since we and our children are driven forth from our dwellings?" But when fighting was commanded them, they turned back, save a few of them: But God knew the offenders!

2:248 And their prophet said to them, "Not hath God set (Talout) Saul king over you." They said, "How shall he reign over us, when we are more worthy of the kingdom than he, and of wealth he hath no abundance?" He said, "Verily God hath chosen him to be over you, and hath given him increase in knowledge and stature; God giveth his kingdom to whom he pleaseth; and God is Liberal, Knowing!"

2:249 And their prophet said to them, "Verily, the sign of his kingship shall be that the Ark shall come to you: in it is a pledge of security from your Lord and the relics left by the family of Moses, and the family of Aaron; the <u>angels</u> shall bear it: Truly herein shall be a sign indeed to you if you are believers."

Sura 2:280-285 - Apostles believeth in God's Angels

2:280 If any one find difficulty in discharging a debt, then let there be a delay until it be easy for him: but if you remit it as alms it will be better for you, if you knew it.

2:281 Fear the day wherein you shall return to God: then shall every soul be rewarded according to its desert, and none shall have injustice done to them.

2:282 O you who believe! when you contract a debt (payable) at a fixed date, write it down, and let the notary faithfully note between you: and let not the notary refuse to note, even as God hath taught him; but let him note it down, and let him who oweth the debt dictate, and let him fear God his Lord, and not diminish aught thereof. But if he who oweth the debt be foolish or weak, or be not able to dictate himself, let his friend dictate for him with fairness; and call to witness two witnesses of your people: but if there be not two men, let there be a man, and two women of those whom you shall judge fit for witnesses: if the one of them should mistake, the other may cause her to recollect. And the witnesses shall not refuse, whenever they shall be summoned. And disdain not to put the debt in writing, be it large or small, with its time of payment: this will be more just for you in the sight of God, better suited for witnessing, and the best for avoiding doubt. But if the goods be there present, and you pass them from hand to hand – then it shall be no fault in you not to write it down. And have witnesses when you sell, and harm not writer or witness: it will be a crime in you to do this. But fear God and God will give you knowledge, for God hath knowledge of all things.

2:283 And if you be on a journey and shall find no notary, let pledges be taken: but if one of you trust the other, let him who is trusted, restore what he is trusted with, and fear God his Lord. And refuse not to give evidence. He who refuseth is surely wicked at heart: and God knoweth your deeds.

2:284 Whatever is in the Heavens and in the Earth is God's: and whether you bring forth to light what is in your minds or conceal it, God will reckon with you for it; and whom He pleaseth will He forgive, and whom He pleaseth will He punish; for God is All-powerful.

2:285 The apostle believeth in that which hath been sent down from his Lord, as do the faithful also. Each one believeth in God, and His Angels, and His Books, and His Apostles: we make no distinction between any of His Apostles. And they say, "We have heard and we obey. Thy mercy, Lord! for unto thee must we return."

Sura 3 Al-Imran (Family of Imran)

Sura 3:10-17 - Angels proclaim "There is no God but He, the Mighty, the Wise"

3:10 Say to the infidels: you shall be worsted, and to Hell shall you be gathered together; and wretched the couch!

3:11 You have already had a sign in the meeting of the two hosts. The one host fought in the cause of God, and the other was infidel. To their own eyesight, the infidels saw you twice as many as themselves:

3:12 And God aided with his succour whom He would: And in this truly was a lesson for men endued with discernment.

3:13 Fair-seeming to men is the love of pleasures from women and children, and the treasured treasures of God and silver, and horses of mark, and flocks, and cornfields! Such the enjoyment of this world's life. But God! goodly the home with Him.

3:14 Say: Shall I tell you of better things than these, prepared for those who fear God, in His presence? Theirs shall be gardens, beneath whose pavilions the rivers flow, and in which shall they abide for aye: and wives of stainless purity, and acceptance with God: for God regardeth his servants –

3:15 Who say, "O our Lord! we have indeed believed; pardon us our sins, and keep us from the torment of the fire;" – The patient, and the truthful, the lowly, and the charitable, and they who seek pardon at each daybreak.

3:16 God witnesseth that there is no god but He: and the <u>angels</u>, and mean endued with knowledge, stablished in righteousness, proclaim "There is no god but He, the Mighty, the Wise!"

3:17 The true religion with God is Islam: and they to whom the Scriptures had been given, differed not till after "the knowledge" had come to them, and through mutual jealousy. But as for him who shall not believe in the signs of God – God will be prompt to reckon with him! If they shall dispute with thee, then Say: I have surrendered myself to God, as have they who follow me.

Sura 3:30-43 - Angels call to Zacharias about his son John as he stood praying in the sanctuary

3:30 Verily above all human beings did God choose Adam, and Noah, and the family of Abraham, and the family of Imran, the one the posterity of the other: And God Heareth, Knoweth.

3:31 Remember when the wife of Imran said, "O my Lord! I vow to thee what is in my womb, for thy special service. Accept it from me, for thou Hearest, Knowest!" And when she had given birth to it, she said, "O my Lord! Verily I have brought forth a female," – God knew what she had brought forth; a male is not as a female – "and I have named her Mary, and I take refuge with thee for her and for her offspring, from Satan the stoned."

3:32 So with goodly acceptance did her Lord accept her, and with goodly growth did he make her grow. Zacharias reared her. So oft as Zacharias went in to Mary at the sanctuary, he found her supplied with food. "Oh, Mary!" said he, "whence hast thou this?" She said, "It is from God; for God supplieth whom He will, without reckoning!"

3:33 There did Zacharias call upon his Lord: "O my Lord!" said he, "vouchsafe me from thyself good descendants, for thou art the hearer of prayer." Then did the angels call to him, as he stood praying in the sanctuary.:

3:34 "God announceth John (Yahia) to thee, who shall be a verifier of the word from God, and a greater one, chaste, and a prophet of the number of the just."

3:35 He said, "O my Lord! how shall I have a son, now that old age hath come upon me, and my wife is barren?" He said, "Thus will God do His pleasure."

3:36 He said, "Lord! give me a token." He said, "Thy token shall be, that for three days thou shalt speak to no man but by signs: But remember thy Lord often, and praise him at even and at morn:"

3:37 And remember when the angels said, "O Mary! verily hath God chosen thee, and purified thee, and chosen thee above the women of the worlds!

3:38 O Mary! be devout towards thy Lord, and prostrate thyself, and bow down with those who bow."

3:39 This is one of the announcements of things unseen by thee: To thee, O Muhammad! do we reveal it; for thou wast not with them when they cast lots with reeds which of them should rear Mary; nor wast thou with them when they disputed about it.

3:40 Remember when the <u>angel</u> said, "O Mary! Verily God announceth to thee the Word from Him: His name shall be, Messiah Jesus the son of Mary, illustrious in this world, and in the next, and one of those who have near access to God;

3:41 And He shall speak to men alike when in the cradle and when grown up; And he shall be one of the just."

3:42 She said, "How, O my Lord! shall I have a son, when man hath not touched me?" He said, "Thus: God will create why He will; When He decreeth a thing, He only saith, 'Be,' and it is."

3:43 And he will teach him the Book, and the Wisdom, and the Law, and the Evangel; and he shall be an apostle to the children of Israel. "Now have I come," he will say, "to you with a sign from your Lord: Out of clay will I make for you, as it were, the figure of a bird: and I will breathe into it, and it shall become, by God's leave, a bird. And I will heal the blind, and the leper; and by God's leave will I quicken the dead; and I will tell you what you eat, and what you store up in your houses! Truly in this will be a sign for you, if you are believers.

Sura 3:70-76 - God doth not command you to take the Angels or prophets as lords

3:70 But whoso is true to his engagement, and feareth God, – verily God loveth those that fear Him.

3:71 Verily they who barter their engagement with God, and their oaths, for some paltry price – These! no portion for them in the world to come! and God will not speak to them, and will not look on them, on the day of resurrection, and will not assoil them! for them, a grievous chastisement!

3:72 And some truly are there among them who torture the Scriptures with their tongues, in order that you may suppose it to be from the Scripture, yet it is not from the Scripture. And they say, "This is from God;" yet it is not from God: and they utter a lie against God, and they know they do so.

3:73 It beseemeth not a man, that God should give him the Scriptures and the Wisdom, and the gift of prophecy, and that then he should say to his followers, "Be you worshippers of me, as well as of God;" but rather, "Be you perfect in things pertaining to God, since you know the Scriptures, and have studied deep."

3:74 God doth not command you to take the angels or the prophets as lord. What! would he command you to become infidels after you have been Muslims?

3:75 When God entered into covenant with the prophets, he said, "This is the Book and the Wisdom which I give you. Hereafter shall a prophet come unto you to confirm the Scriptures already with you. You shall surely believe on him, and you shall surely aid him. Are you resolved?" said he, "and do you accept the covenant on these terms?" They said, "We are resolved;" "Be you then the witnesses," said he, "and I will be a witness as well as you.

3:76 And whoever turneth back after this, these are surely the perverse."

Sura 3:80-83 - The recompense of Angels are on the disbelieving

3:80 How shall God guide a people who, after they had believed and bore witness that the apostle was true, and after that clear proofs of his mission had reached them, disbelieved? God guideth not the people who transgress.

3:81 These! their recompense, that the curse of God, and of angels, and of all men, is on them!

3:82 Under it shall they abide for ever; their torment shall not be assuaged! nor shall God even look upon them! –

3:83 Save those who after this repent and amend; for verily God is Gracious, Merciful!

Sura 3:120-126 - The faithful will be aideth with three thousand angels but the steadfast will help with five thousand angels

3:120 Then thou didst say to the faithful, "is it not enough for you that your Lord aideth you with three thousand <u>angels</u> sent down from on high?"

3:121 Aye: but if you be steadfast and fear God, and the foe come upon you in hot haste, your Lord will help you with five thousand <u>angels</u> in their cognisances!

3:122 This, as pure good tidings for you, did God appoint, that your hearts might be assured – for only from God, the Mighty, the Wise, cometh the Victory - and that He might cut off the uttermost part of those who the Victory - and that He might cut off the uttermost part of those who believed not, or cast them down so that they should be overthrown, defeated without resource.

3:123 It is none of thy concern whether He be turned unto them in kindness or chastise them: for verily they are wrongful doers.

3:124 Whatever is in the Heavens and the Earth is God's! He forgiveth whom He will, and whom He will, chastiseth: for God is Forgiving, Merciful.

3:125 O you who believe! devour not usury, doubling it again and again!

3:126 But fear God, that you may prosper.

Sura 4 Al-An-Nisa (Women)

Sura 4:99-100 - Angels took the souls of the unjust

4:99 The <u>angels</u>, when they took the souls of those who had been unjust to their own weal, demanded, "What hath been your state?"

They said, "We were the weak ones of the earth." They replied, "Was not God's earth broad enough for you to flee away in?" These! their home shall be Hell, and evil the passage to it –

4:100 Except the men and women and children who were not able, through their weakness, to find the mean of escape, and were not guided on their way. These haply God will forgive: for God is Forgiving, Gracious.

Sura 4:130-137 - Whoever believeth not on God and His angels hath erred

4:130 And whatever is in the Heavens and in the Earth is God's! We have already enjoined those to whom the Scriptures were given before you, and yourselves, to fear God. But if you become unbelievers, yet know that whatever is in the Heavens and in the Earth is God's: and God is Rich, Praiseworthy.

4:131 All that is in Heaven and all that is in Earth is God's! God is a sufficient protector!

4:132 If he pleased, he could cause you to pass away, O mankind! and create others in your stead: for this hath God power.

4:133 If any one desire the reward of this world, yet with God is the reward of this world and of the next! And God Heareth, Beholdeth.

4:134 O you who believe! stand fast to justice, when you bear witness

4:135 O you who believe! stand fast to justice, when you bear witness before God, though it be against yourselves, or your parents, or your kindred, whether the party be rich or poor. God is nearer than you to both. Therefore follow not passion, lest you swerve from truth. And if you wrest your testimony or stand aloof, God verily is well aware of what you do.

4:136 O you who believe! believe in God and his Apostle, and the Book which he hath sent down to his Apostle, and the Book which he hath sent down aforetime. Whoever believeth not on God and his Angels and his Books and his Apostles, and in the last day, he verily hath erred with far-gone error.

4:137 Verily, they who believed, then became unbelievers, then believed, and against became unbelievers, and then increased their unbelief – it is not God who will forgive them or guide them into the way.

Sura 4:160-164 - The angels are also witnesses to what God hath sent down

4:160 But their men of solid knowledge, and the believers who believe in that which hath been sent down to thee, and in what hath been sent down before thee, and who observe prayer, and pay the alms of obligation, and believe in God and the latter day, – these! we will give them a great reward.

4:161 Verily we have revealed to thee as we revealed to Noah and the Prophets after him, and as we revealed to Abraham, and Ismauel and Isaac, and Jacob, and the tribes, and Jesus, and Job, and Jonah, and Aaron, and Solomon; and to David gave we Psalms.

4:162 Of some apostles we have told thee before: of other apostles we have not told thee – And discoursing did God discourse with Moses.

4:163 Apostles charged to announce and to warn, that men, after those apostles, might have no plea against god. And God is Mighty, Wise!

4:164 But God is himself witness of what He hath sent down to thee: In His knowledge hath He sent it down to thee. The angels are also its witnesses: but God is a sufficient witness!

Sura 4:170-171 - The angels disdaineth not to be a servant of God

4:170 The Messiah disdaineth not to be a servant of God, nor do the angels who are nigh unto Him.

4:171 And whoso disdaineth His service, and is filled with pride, God will gather them all to Himself.

Sura 6 Al-Anam (Cattle)

Sura 6:1-9 - Unless an angel sent down (the Book) to him... if we had appointed an angel, we would have appointed one in the form of a man

6:1 Praise be to God, who hath created the Heavens and the Earth, and ordained the darkness and the light! Yet unto their Lord do the infidels give peers!

6:2 He it is who created you of clay – then decreed the term of your life: and with Him is another prefixed term for the resurrection. Yet have you doubts thereof!

6:3 And He is God in the Heavens and on the Earth! He knoweth your secrets and your disclosures! and He knoweth what you deserve.

6:4 Never did one single sign from among the signs of their Lord come to them, but they turned away from it;

6:5 And now, after it hath reached them, have they treated the truth itself as a lie. But in the end, a message as to that which they have mocked, shall reach them.

6:6 See they not how many generations we have destroyed before them? We had settled them on the earth as we have not settled you, and we sent down the very heavens upon them in copious rains, and we made the rivers to flow beneath their feet: yet we destroyed them in their sins, and raised up other generations to succeed them.

6:7 And had we sent down to thee a Book written on parchment, and they had touched it with their hands, the infidels had surely said, "This is nought but plain sorcery."

6:8 They say, too, "Unless an <u>angel</u> be sent down to him...." But if we had sent down an <u>angel</u>, their judgment would have come on them at once, and they would have had no respite:

6:9 And if we had appointed an <u>angel</u>, we should certainly have appointed one in the form of a man, and we should have clothed him before them in garments like their own.

Sura 6:48-52 - Neither do I say to you, "Verily, I am an Angel"

6:48 We send not our Sent Ones but as heralds of good news and warners; and whoso shall believe and amend, on them shall come no fear, neither shall they be sorrowful:

6:49 But whoso shall charge our signs with falsehood, on them shall fall a punishment for their wicked doings.

6:50 Say: I say not to you, "In my possession are the treasures of God;" neither say I, "I know things secret;" neither do I say to you, "Verily, I am an <u>angel</u>:" Only what is revealed to me do I follow. Say: Shall the blind and the seeing be esteemed alike? Will you not then reflect?

6:51 And warn those who dread their being gathered to their Lord, that patron or intercessor they shall have none but Him, – to the intent that they may fear Him!

6:52 And thrust not thou away those who cry to their Lord at morn and even, craving to behold his face. It is not for thee in anything to judge of their motives, nor for them in anything to judge of thee. If thou thrust them away thou wilt be of the doers of wrong.

Sura 6:90-93 - The angels reach forth their hands saying, "yield up your souls …"

6:90 These are they whom God hath guided: follow therefore their guidance. Say: No pay do I ask of you for this: Verily it is no other than the teaching for all creatures.

6:91 No just estimate do they form of God when they say, "Nothing hath God sent down to man." Say: Who sent down the Book which Moses brought, a light and guidance to man, which you set down on paper, publishing part, but concealing most; though you have now been taught that which neither you nor your fathers knew? Say: It is God: then leave them in their pastime of cavillings.

6:91 And this Book which we have sent down is blessed, confirming that which was before it; and in order that thou mightest warn the mothercity and those who dwell round about it. They who believe in the next life will believe in It, and will keep strictly to their Prayers.

6:93 But is any more wicked than he who deviseth a lie of God, or saith, "I have had a revelation," when nothing was revealed to him? And who saith, "I can bring down a book like that which God hath sent down"? But couldst thou see when the ungodly are in the floods of death, and the <u>angels</u> reach forth their hands saying, "Yield up your souls: – this day shall you be recompensed with a humiliating punishment for your untrue sayings about God, and for proudly rejecting his signs!"

Sura 6:110-114 - Though we had sent down the angels to them, they had not believed

6:110 And we will turn their hearts and their eyes away from the truth, because they did not believe therein at first, and we will leave them in their transgressions, wandering in perplexity.

6:111 And though we had sent down the <u>angels</u> to them, and the dead had spoken to them, and we had gathered all things about them in tribes, they had not believed, unless God had willed it! but most of them do not know it.

6:112 Thus have we given an enemy to every prophet – Satans among men and among Djinn: tinsel discourses do they suggest the one to the other, in order to deceive: and had they Lord willed it, they would not have done it. Therefore, leave them and their vain imaginings –

6:113 And let the hearts of those who believe not in the life to come incline thereto, and let them find their content in this, and let them gain what they are gaining.

6:114 What! shall I seek other judge than God, when it is He who hath sent down to you the distinguishing Book? They to whom we have given the Book know that it is sent down from thy Lord with truth. Be not thou then of those we doubt.

Sura 6:155-159 - What wait they for, but the coming of the angels to them

6:155 Then gave we the Book to Moses – complete for him who should do right, and a decision for all matters, and a guidance, and a mercy, that they might believe in the meeting with their Lord.

6:156 Blessed, too, this Book which we have sent down. Wherefore follow it and fear God, that you may find mercy: Lest you should say, "The Scriptures were indeed sent down only unto two peoples before us, but we were not able to go deep into their studies:"

6:157 Or lest you should say, "If a book had been sent down to us, we had surely followed the guidance better than they." But now hath a clear exposition come to you from your Lord, and a guidance and a mercy.

6:158 Who then is more wicked than he who treateth the signs of God as lies, and turneth aside from them? We will recompense those who turn aside from our signs with an evil punishment, because they have turned aside.

6:159 What wait they for, but the coming of the angels to them, or the coming of thy Lord Himself, or that some of the signs of thy Lord should come to pass? On the day when some of thy Lord's signs shall come to pass, its faith shall not profit a soul which believed not before, nor wrought good works in virtue of its faith. Say: Wait you. Verily, we will wait also.

Sura 7 Al-A'Raf (The Heights)

Sura 7:10-18 - We said to the angels, "Prostrate yourselves unto Adam" and they did, save Elbis

7:10 We created you; then fashioned you; then said we to the angels, "Prostrate yourselves unto Adam: and they prostrated them all in worship, save Ebilis: He was not among those who prostrated themselves.

7:11 To him said God: "What hath hindered thee from prostrating thyself in worship at my bidding?" He said, "Nobler am I than he: me hast thou created of fire; of clay hast thou created him."

7:12 He said, "Get thee down hence: Paradise is no place for thy pride: Get thee gone then; one of the despised shalt thou be."

7:13 He said, "Respite me till the day when mankind shall be raised from the dead."

7:14 He said, "One of the respited shalt thou be."

7:15 He said, "Now, for that thou hast caused me to err, surely in thy straight path will I lay wait for them:

7:16 Then I will surely come upon them from before, and from behind, and from their right hand, and from their left, and thou shalt not find the greater part of them to be thankful."

7:17 He said, "Go forth from it, a scorned, a banished one! Whoever of them shall follow thee, I will surely fill hell with you, one and all.

7:18 And, O Adam! dwell thou and thy wife in Paradise, and eat you whence you will, but to this tree approach not, lest you become of the unjust doers."

Sura 7:19 - Satan said, "This tree hath your Lord forbidden you, only lest ye should become angels, or ... immortals"

7:19 Then Satan whispered them to shew them their nakedness, which had been hidden from them both. And he said, "This tree hath your Lord forbidden you, only lest you should become <u>angels</u>, or lest you should become immortals."

Sura 8 Al-Anfal (The Spoils)

Sura 8:1-10 - The Lord answered you, "I will verily aid you with a thousand angels, rank on rank"

8:1 They will question thee about the Spoils. Say: The spoils are God's and the apostle's. Therefore, fear God, and settle this among yourselves; and obey God and his apostle, if you are believers.

8:2 Believers are they only whose hearts thrill with fear when God is named, and whose faith increaseth at each recital of his signs, and who put their trust in their Lord;

8:3 Who observe the prayers, and give alms out of that with which we have supplied them;

8:4 These are the believers: their due grade awaiteth them in the presence of their Lord, and forgiveness, and a generous provision.

8:5 Remember how thy Lord caused thee to go forth from thy home on a mission of truth, and part of the believers were quite averse to it:

8:6 They disputed with thee about the truth which had been made so clear, as if they were being led forth to death, and saw it before them:

8:7 And remember when God promised you that one of the two troops should fall to you, and you desired that they who had no arms should fall to you: but God purposed to prove the truth of his words, and to cut off the uttermost part of the infidels;

8:8 That he might prove his truth to be the truth, and bring nought that which is nought, though the impious were averse to it:

8:9 When you sought succour of your Lord, and he answered you, "I will verily aid you with a thousand angels, rank on rank:"

8:10 And God made this promise as pure good tidings, and to assure your hearts by it: for succour cometh from God alone! Verily God is Mighty, Wise.

Sura 8:11-19 - Thy Lord spake unto the angels, "I will be with you: therefore stablish ye the faithful'"

8:11 Recollect when sleep, a sign of security from Him, fell upon you, and he sent down upon you water from Heaven that he might thereby cleanse you, and cause the pollution of Satan to pass from you, and that he might gird up your hearts, and stablish your feet by it:

8:12 When thy Lord spake unto the angels, "I will be with you: therefore stablish you the faithful. I will cast a dread into the hearts of the infidels." Strike off their heads then, and strike off from them every finger-tip.

8:13 This, because they have opposed God and his apostle: And whoso shall oppose God and his apostle.... Verily, God will be severe in punishment.

8:14 "This for you! Taste it then! and for the infidels is the tortue of the fire!"

8:15 O you who believe! when you meet the marshalled hosts of the infidels, turn not your backs to them:

8:16 Whoso shall turn his back to them on that day, unless he turn aside to fight, or to rally to some other troop, shall incur wrath from God: Hell shall be his abode and wretched the journey thither!

8:17 So it was not you who slew them, but God slew them; and those shafts were God's not thine! He would make trial of the faithful by a gracious trial from Himself: Verily, God Heareth, Knoweth.

8:18 This befel, that God might also bring to nought the craft of the infidels.

8:19 O Meccans! if you desired a decision, now hath the decision come to you. It will be better for you if you give over the struggle. If you return to it, we will return; and your forces, though they be many, shall never avail you aught, for God is with the faithful.

Sura 8:50-53 - The angels cause the infidels to die!

8:50 When Satan prepared their works for them, and said, "No man shall conquer you this day; and verily I will be near to help you:" But when the two armies came in sight, he turned on his heel and said, "Ay, I am clear of you: ay, I see what you see now: ay, I fear God; for God is severe in punishing."

8:51 When the hypocrites and the diseased of heart said, "Their Religion hath misled the Muslims: But whoso putteth his trust in God.... Yes, verily God is Mighty, Wise!

8:52 If thou didst see, when the angels cause the infidels to die! They smite their faces and their backs, and – "Taste you the torture of the burning:

8:53 This, for what your hands have sent on before you:" – God is not unjust to his servants.

Sura 11 Hud

Sura 11:10-17 - If an angel come with him

11:10 And if thou say, "After death you shall surely be raised again," the infidels will certainly explain, "This is nothing but pure sorcery."

11:11 And if we defer their chastisement to some definite time, they will exclaim, "What keepeth it back?" What! will it not come upon them on a day when there shall be none to avert it from them? And that at which they scoffed shall enclose them in on every side.

11:12 And if we cause man to taste our mercy, and then deprive him of it, verily, he is despairing, ungrateful.

11:13 And if after trouble hath befallen him we cause him to taste our favour, he will surely exclaim, "The evils are passed away from me."

11:14 Verily, he is joyous, boastful.

11:15 Except those who endure with patience and do the things that are right: these doth pardon await and a great reward.

11:16 Perhaps thou wilt suppress a part of what hath been revealed to thee, and wilt be distressed at heart lest they say, "If a treasure be not sent down to him, or an <u>angel</u> come with him...." But thou art only a warner, and God hath all things in his charge.

11:17 If they shall say, "The Koran is his own device," Say: Then bring ten Suras like it of your devising, and call whom you can to your aid beside God, if you are men of truth.

Sura 11:30-33 - Nor do I say, "I am an angel"

11:30 He said: "O my people! how think you? If I am upon a clear revelation from my Lord, who hath bestowed on me mercy from Himself to which you are blind, can we force it on you, if you are averse from it?

11:31 And, O my people! I ask you not for riches: my reward is of God alone: and I will not drive away those who believe that they shall meet their Lord: – but I see that you are an ignorant people.

11:32 And, O my people! were I to drive them away, who shall help me against God? Will you not therefore consider?

11:33 And I tell you not that with me are the treasurers of God: nor do I say, 'I know the things unseen;' nor do I say, 'I am an <u>angel</u>;' nor do I say of those whom you eye with scorn, No good thing will God bestow on them: – God best knoweth what is in their minds – for then should I be one of those who act unjustly."

Sura 11:80-85 - The Angels tell Lot they are messengers of the Lord and to depart in the dead of night

11:80 And his people came rushing on towards him, for aforetime had they wrought this wickedness. He said, "O my people! these my daughters will be purer for you: fear God, and put me not to shame in my guests. Is there no rightminded man among you?"

11:81 They said, "Thou knowest now that we need not thy daughters; and thou well knowest what we require."

11:82 He said, "Would that I had strength to resist you, or that I could find refuge with some powerful chieftain."

11:83 The <u>Angels</u> said, "O Lot! verily, we are the messengers of thy Lord: they shall not touch tee: depart with thy family in the dead of night, and let not one of you turn back: as for thy wife, on her shall light what shall light on them. Verily, that with which they are threatened is for the morning. Is not the morning near?"

11:84 And when our decree came to be executed we turned those cities upside down, and we rained down upon them blocks of claystone one after another, marked by thy Lord himself. Nor are they far distant from the wicked Meccans.

11:85 And we sent to Madian their brother Shoaib. He said, "O my people! worship God: no other God have you than He: give not short weight and measure: I see indeed that you revel in good things; but I fear for you the punishment of the all-encompassing day.

Sura 12 Yusuf (Joseph)

Sura 12:30-34 - Joseph being called a noble angel

12:30 And in the city, the women said, "The wife of the Prince hath solicited her servant: he hath fired her with his love: but we clearly see her manifest error."

12:31 And when she heard of their cabal, she sent to them and got ready a banquet for them, and gave each one of them a knife, and said, "Joseph shew thyself to them." And when they saw him they were amazed at him, and cut their hands, and said, "God keep us! This is no man! This is no other than a noble <u>angel</u>!"

12:32 She said, "This is he about whom you blamed me. I wished him to yield to my desires, but he stood firm. But if he obey not my command, he shall surely be cast into prison, and become one of the despised."

12:33 He said, "O my Lord! I prefer the prison to compliance with their bidding: but unless thou turn away their snares from me, I shall play the youth with them, and become one of the unwise."

12:34 And his Lord heard him and turned aside their snares from him: for he is the Hearer, the Knower.

Sura 13 Ar-Rad (The Thunder)

Sura 13:10-12 - Each hath a succession of Angels before him and behind him, who watch over him by God's behest

13:10 Knower of the Hidden and the Manifest! the Great! the Most High!

13:11 Alike to Him is that person among you who concealeth his words, and he that telleth them abroad: he who hideth him in the night, and he who cometh forth in the day.

13:12 Each hath a succession of Angels before him and behind him, who watch over him by God's behest. Verily, God will not change his gifts to men, till they change what is in themselves: and when God willeth evil unto men, there is none can turn it away, nor have they any protector beside Him.

Sura 13:13-19 - The Angels uttereth His praise for awe of Him

13:13 He it is who maketh the lightning to shine unto you; for fear and hope: and who bringeth up the laden clouds.

13:14 And the Thunder uttereth his praise, and the Angels also, for awe of Him: and he sendeth his bolts and smiteth with them whom he will while they are wrangling about God! Mighty is he is prowess.

13:15 Prayer is His of right: but these deities to whom they pray beside Him give them no answer, otherwise than as he is answered who stretcheth forth his hands to the water that it may reach his mouth, when it cannot reach it! The prayer of the Infidels only wandereth, and is lost.

13:16 And unto God doth all in the Heavens and on the Earth bow down in worship, willingly or by constraint: their very shadows also morn and even!

13:17 Say: Who is Lord of the Heavens and of the Earth? Say: God. Say: Why then have you taken beside Him protectors, who even for their own selves have no power for help or harm? Say: What! shall the blind and the seeing be held equal? Shall the darkness and the light be held equal? Or have they given associates to God who have created as He hath created, so that their creation appear to them like His? Say: God is the Creator of all things! He is the One! the Conquering!

13:18 He sendeth down the rain from Heaven: then flow the torrents in their due measure, and the flood beareth along a swelling foam. And from the metals which are molten in the fire for the sake of ornaments or utensils, a like scum ariseth. In this way doth God depict (set forth) truth and falsehood. As to the foam, it is quickly gone: and as to what is useful to man, it remaineth on the earth,. Thus doth God set forth comparisons! To those who respond to their Lord shall be an excellent reward; but those who respond not to his call, had they all that the earth containeth twice over, they would surely give it for their ransom. Evil their reckoning! and Hell their home! And wretched the bed!

13:19 Shall he then who knoweth that what hath been sent down to thee from thy Lord is the truth, act like him who is blind? Men of insight only will bear this in mind.

Sura 13:20-24 - And the angels shall go in unto them at every portal

13:20 Who fulfil their pledge to God, and break not their compact: And who join together what God hath bidden to be joined, and who fear their Lord, and dread an ill reckoning;

13:21 And who, from desire to see the face of their Lord, are constant amid trials, and observe prayer and give alms, in secret and openly, out of what we have bestowed upon them, and turn aside evil by good: for these is the recompense of that abode.

13:22 Gardens of Eden – into which they shall enter together with the just of their fathers, and their wives, and their descendants: and the angels shall go in unto them at every portal:

13:23 "Peace be with you!" say they, "because you have endured all things!" charming the recompense of their abode!

13:24 But those who, after having contracted it, break their covenant with God, and cut asunder what God hath bidden to be united, and commit misdeeds on the earth, these, a curse awaiteth them, and an ill abode!

Sura 15 Al-Hijr

Sura 15:1-14 - Wouldst thou not have come to us with the angels ... We will not send down the angels without due cause

15:1 Elif. Lam. Ra. These are the signs of the Book, and of a lucid recital [Koran].

15:2 Many a time will the infidels wish that they had been Muslims.

15:3 Let them feast and enjoy themselves, and let hope beguile them: but they shall know the truth at last.

15:4 We never destroyed a city whose term was not perfixed:

15:5 No people can forstall or retard its destiny.

15:6 They say: "O thou to whom the warning hath been sent down, thou art surely possessed by a djinn:

15:7 Wouldst thou not have come to us with the angels, if thou wert of those who assert the truth?"

15:8 We will not send down the angels without due cause. The Infidels would not in that case have been respited.

15:9 Verily, We have sent down the warning, and verily, We will be its guardian;

15:10 And already have We sent Apostles, before thee, among the sects of the ancients;

15:11 But never came Apostles to them whom they did not deride. In like manner will We put it into the hearts of the sinners of Mecca to do the same:

15:12 They will not believe on him though the example of those of old hath gone before.

15:13 Even were We to open above them a gate in Heaven, yet all the while they were mounting up to is,

15:14 They would surely say: It is only that our eyes are drunken: nay, we are a people enchanted.

Sura 15:28-35 - The Lord said to the Angels, "I created man…" and the angels bowed down in worship … save Eblis

15:28 Remember when thy Lord said to the <u>Angels</u>, "I create man of dried clay, of dark loam moulded:

15:29 And when I shall have fashioned him and breathed of my spirit into him, then fall you down and worship him."

15:30 And the <u>Angels</u> bowed down in worship, all of them, all together, Save Eblis: he refused to be with those who bowed in worship.

15:31 "O Eblis," said God, "wherefore art thou not with those who bow down in worship?"

15:32 He said, "It beseemeth not me to bow in worship to man whom thou hast created of clay, of moulded loam."

15:33 He said, "Begone then hence; thou art a stoned one,

15:34 And the curse shall be on thee till the day of reckoning."

15:35 He said, "O my Lord! respite me till the day when man shall be raised from the dead."

Sura 16 An-Nahl (The Bee)

Sura 16:1-3 - By His own behest will He cause the angels to descend with the Spirit on whom he leaseth among his servants

16:1 The doom of God cometh to pass. Then hasten it not. Glory be to Him! High let Him be exalted above the gods whom they joint with Him!

16:2 But His own behest will He cause the angels to descend with the Spirit on whom he pleaseth among his servants, bidden them, "Warn that there is no God but me; therefore fear me."

16:3 He hath created the Heavens and the Earth to set forth his truth; high let Him be exalted above the gods they join with Him!

Sura 16:30-31 - The sinners against their own souls whom the angels shall cause to die

16:30 They are sinners against their own souls whom the angels shall cause to die will proffer the submission, "No evil have we done." Nay! God knoweth what you have wrought:

16:31 Enter you therefore the gates of Hell to remain therein for ever: and horrid the abiding place of the haughty ones!

Sura 16:32-34 - As righteous persons, the angels shall say when they receive their soul, "Peace be on you!"

16:32 But to those who have feared God it shall be said, "What is this that your Lord hath awarded?" They shall say, "That which is best. To those who do good, a good reward in this present world; but better the mansion of the next, and right pleasant the abode of the Godfearing!"

16:33 Gardens of Eden into which they shall enter; rivers shall flow beneath their shades; all they wish for shall they find therein! Thus God rewardeth those who fear Him:

16:34 To whom, as righteous persons, the <u>angels</u> shall say, when they receive their souls, "Peace be on you! Enter Paradise as the meed of your labours."

Sura 16:35-38 - What can the infidels expect but that the angels of death come upon them

16:35 What can the infidels expect but that the <u>angels</u> of death come upon them, or that a sentence of thy Lord take effect? Thus did they who flourished before them. God was not unjust to them, but to their ownselves were they unjust; and the ill which they had done recoiled upon them, and that which they had scoffed at encompassed them round about.

16:36 They who have joined other gods with God say, "Had he pleased, neither we nor our fathers had worshipped aught but him; nor should we, apart from him, have forbidden aught." Thus acted they who were before them. Yet is the duty of the apostles other than public preaching?

16:37 And to every people have we sent an apostle saying: – Worship God and turn away from false gods. Some of them there were whom God guided, and there were others decreed to err. But go through the land and see what hath been the end of those who treated my apostles as liars!

16:38 If thou art anxious for their guidance, know that God will not guide him whom He would lead astray, neither shall they have any helpers.

Sura 16:50-56 - The very angels, prostrate them in adoration before God, and are free from pride

16:50 Have they not seen how everything which God hath created turneth its shadow right and left, prostrating itself before God in all abasement?

16:50 And all in the Heavens and all on the Earth, each thing that moveth, and the very <u>angels</u>, prostrate them in adoration before God, and are free from pride;

16:51 They fear their Lord who is above them, and do what they are bidden:

16:52 For God hath said, "Take not to yourselves two gods, – for He is one God: me, therefore! yea, me revere!

16:53 All in the Heavens and in the Earth is His! His due unceasing service! Will you then fear any other than God?

16:54 And all your blessings are assuredly from God: then, when trouble befalleth you, to Him you turn for help:

16:55 Then when He relieveth you of the trouble, lo! some of you join associates with your Lord: –

16:56 To prove how thankless are they for our gifts! Enjoy yourselves then: but in the end you shall know the truth.

Sura 17 Bani Israil (The Children of Israel)

Sura 17:40-44 - Hath your Lord taken for himself daughters from among the angels?

17:40 All this is evil; odious to thy Lord.

17:41 This is a part of the wisdom which thy Lord hath revealed to thee. Set not up any other god with God, lest thou be cast into Hell, rebuked, cast away.

17:42 What! hath your Lord prepared sons for you, and taken for himself daughters from among the angels? Indeed, you say a dreadful saying.

17:43 Moreover, for man's warning have we varied this Koran: Yet it only increaseth their flight from it.

17:44 Say: If, as you affirm, there were other gods with Him, they would in that case seek occasion against the occupant of the throne: Glory to Him! Immensely high is He exalted above their blasphemies!

Sura 17:60-67 - We said to the Angels, "Prostrate yourselves before Adam"

17:60 There is no city which we will not destroy before the day of Resurrection, or chastise it with a grievous chastisement. This is written in the Book.

17:61 Nothing hindered us from sending thee with the power of working miracles, except that the people of old treated them as lies. We gave to Themoud the she-camel before their very eyes, yet they maltreated her! We send not a prophet with miracles but to strike terror.

17:62 And remember when we said to thee, Verily, thy Lord is round about mankind; we ordained the vision which we shewed thee, and likewise the cursed tree of the Koran, only for men to dispute of; we will strike them with terror; but it shall only increase in them enormous wickedness:

17:63 And when we said to the <u>Angels</u>, "Prostrate yourselves before Adam:" and they all prostrated them, save Eblis. "What!" said he, "shall I bow me before him whom thou hast created of clay?

17:64 Seest thou this man whom thou hast honoured above me? Verily, if thou respite me till the day of Resurrection, I will destroy his offspring, except a few."

17:65 He say, "Begone: but whosoever of them shall follow thee, verily, Hell shall be your recompense; an ample recompense!

17:66 And entice such of them as thou canst by thy voice; assault them with thy horsemen and thy footmen; be their partner in their riches and in their children, and make them promises: but Satan shall make them only deceitful promises.

17:67 As to my servants, no power over them shalt thou have; And thy Lord will be their sufficient guardian."

Sura 17:90-101 - Bring God and the angels to watch for thee … Did angels walk the earth as its familiar, we had surely sent them an angel-apostle out of Heaven

17:90 Say: Verily, were men and Djinn assembled to produce the like of this Koran, they could not produce its like, though the one should help the other.

17:91 And of a truth we have set out to men every kind of similitude in this Koran, but most men have refused everything except unbelief.

17:92 And they say, "By no means will we believe on thee till thou cause a fountain to gush forth for us from the earth;

17:93 Or, till thou have a garden of palm-trees and grapes, and thou cause forth-gushing rivers to gush forth in its midst;

17:94 Or thou make the heaven to fall on us, as thou hast given out, in pieces; or thou bring God and the angels to vouch for thee;

17:95 Or thou have a house of gold; or thou mount up into Heaven; nor will we believe in thy mounting up, till thou send down to us a book which we may read." Say: Praise be to my Lord! Am I more than a man, an apostle?

17:96 And what hindereth men from believing, when the guidance hath come to them, but that they say, "Hath God sent a man as an apostle?"

17:97 Say: Did angels walk the earth as its familiars, we had surely sent them an angel-apostle out of Heaven.

17:98 Say: God is witness enough between you and me. His servants He scanneth, eyeth.

17:99 And He whom God shall guide will be guided indeed; and whom he shall mislead thou shalt find none to assist, but Him: and we will gather them together on the day of the resurrection, on their faces, blind and dumb and deaf: Hell shall be their abode: so oft as its fires die down, we will rekindle the flame.

17:100 This shall be their reward for that they believed not our signs and said, "When we shall have become bones and dust, shall we surely be raised a new creation?"

17:101 Do they not perceive that God, who created the Heavens and the Earth, is able to create their like? And he hath ordained them a term; there is no doubt of it: but the wicked refuse everything except unbelief.

Sura 18 Al-Kahf (The Cave)

Sura 18:40-49 - We said to the angels, "Prostrate yourselves before Adam" and they did, save Eblis

18:40 And his fruits were encompassed by destruction. Then began he to turn down the palms of his hands at what he had spent on it; for its vines were falling down on their trellises, and he said, "Oh that I had not joined any other god to my Lord!"

18:41 And he had no host to help him instead of God, neither was he able to help himself.

18:42 Protection in such a case is of God – the Truth: He is the best rewarder, and He bringeth to the best issue.

18:43 And set before them a similitude of the present life. It is as water which we send down from Heaven, and the herb of the Earth is mingled with it, and on the morrow it becometh dry stubble which the winds scatter: for God hath power over all things.

18:44 Wealth and children are the adornment of this present life: but good works, which are lasting, are better in the sight of thy Lord as to recompense, and better as to hope.

18:45 And call to mind the day when we will cause the mountains to pass away, and thou shalt see the earth a levelled plain, and we will gather mankind together, and not leave of them any one.

18:46 And they shall be set before thy Lord in ranks: – "Now are you come unto us as we created you at first: but you thought that we should not make good to you the promise."

18:47 And each shall have his book put into his hand: and thou shalt see the wicked in alarm at that which is therein: and they shall say, "O woe to us! what meaneth this Book? It leaveth neither small nor great unnoted down!" And they shall find all that they have wrought present to them, and thy Lord will not deal unjustly with any one.

18:48 When we said to the <u>angels</u>, "Prostrate yourselves before Adam," they all prostrated them save Eblis, who was of the Djinn, and revolted from his Lord's behest. – What! will you then take him and his offspring as patrons rather than Me? and they your enemies? Sad exchange for the ungodly!

18:49 I made them not witnesses of the creation of the Heavens and of the Earth, nor of their own creation, neither did I take seducers as my helpers.

Sura 20 Ta Ha

Sura 20:110-119 - We said to the angels, "Fall down and worship Adam" and they did, save Eblis

20:110 And humble shall be their faces before Him that Liveth, the Self-subsisting: and undone he, who shall bear the burden of iniquity;

20:111 But he who shall have done the things that are right and is a believer, shall fear neither wrong nor loss.

20:112 Thus have We sent down to thee an Arabic Koran, and have set forth menaces therein diversely, that haply they may fear God, or that it may give birth to reflection in them.

20:113 Exalted then be God, the King, the Truth! Be not hasty in its recital while the revelation of it to thee is incomplete. Say rather, "O my Lord, increase knowledge unto me."

20:114 And of old We made a covenant with Adam; but he forgat it; and we found no firmness of purpose in him.

20:115 And when We said to the <u>angels</u>, "Fall down and worship Adam," they worshipped all, save Eblis, who refused: and We said, "O Adam! this truly is a foe to thee and to thy wife. Let him not therefore drive you out of the garden, and you become wretched;

20:116 For to thee is it granted that thou shalt not hunger therein, neither shalt thou be naked;

20:117 And that thou shalt not thirst therein, neither shalt thou parch with heat;"

20:118 But Satan whispered him: said he, "O Adam! shall I shew thee the tree of Eternity, and the Kingdom that faileth not?:"

20:119 And they both ate thereof, and their nakedness appeared to them, and they began to sew of the leaves of the Garden to cover them, and Adam disobeyed his Lord and went astray.

Sura 21 Al-Anbiya (The Prophets)

Sura 21:1-24 - The angels say in mockery, "Flee not"

21:1 This people's reckoning hath drawn nigh, yet, sunk in carelessness, they turn aside.

21:2 Every fresh warning that cometh to them from their Lord they only hear to mock it, –

21:3 Their hearts set on lusts: and they who have done this wrong say in secret discourse, "Is He more than a man like yourselves? What! will you, with your eyes open, accede to sorcery?"

21:4 Say: "My Lord knoweth what is spoken in the heaven and on the earth: He is the Hearer, the Knower."

21:5 "Nay," say they, "it is the medley of dreams: nay, he hath forged it: nay, he is a poet: let him come to us with a sign as the prophets of old were sent."

21:6 Before their time, none of the cities which we have destroyed, believed: will these men, then, believe?

21:7 And we sent none, previous to thee, but men to whom we had revealed ourselves. Ask you the people who are warned by

21:8 Scriptures, if you know it not.

21:9 We have them not bodies which could dispense with food: and they were not to live for ever.

21:10 Then made we good our promise to them; and we delivered them and whom we pleased, and we destroyed the transgressors.

21:11 And now have we sent down to you "the book," in which is your warning: What, will you not then understand?

21:12 And how many a guilty city have we broken down, and raised up after it other peoples:

21:13 And when they felt our vengeance, lo! they fled from it.

21:14 "Flee not," said the <u>angels</u> in mockery, "but come back to that wherein you revelled, and to your abodes! Questions will haply be put to you."

21:15 They said, "Oh, woe to us! Verily we have been evil doers."

21:16 And this ceased not to be their cry, until we made them like reaped corn, extinct.

21:17 We created not the heaven and the earth, and what is between them, for sport: Had it been our wish to find a pastime, we had surely found it in ourselves; – if to do so had been our will.

21:18 Nay, we will hurl the truth at falsehood, and it shall smite it, and lo! it shall vanish. But woe be to you for what you utter of God!

21:19 All beings in the heaven and on the earth are His: and they who are in his presence disdain not his service, neither are they wearied:

21:20 They praise Him night and day: they rest not.

21:21 Have they taken gods from the earth who can quicken the dead?

21:22 Had there been in either heaven or earth gods besides God, both surely had gone to ruin. But glory be to God, the Lord of the throne, beyond what they utter!

21:23 He shall not be asked of his doings, but they shall be asked.

21:24 Have they taken other gods beside Him? Say; Bring forth your proofs that they are gods. This is the warning of those who are with me, and the warning of those who were before me: but most of them know not the truth, and turn aside.

Sura 21:25-28 - The God of Mercy hath begotten issue from the angels

21:25 No apostle have we sent before thee to whom we did not reveal that "Verily there is no God beside me: therefore worship me."

21:27 Yet they say, "The God of Mercy hath begotten issue from the <u>angels</u>." Glory be to Him! Nay, they are but His honoured servants: They speak not till He hath spoken; and they do His bidding.

21:28 He knoweth what is before them and what is behind them; and no plea shall they offer.

Sura 21:29- 30 - The angel among them saith "I am a god beside Him"

21:29 Save for whom He pleaseth; and they tremble for fear of Him.

21:30 And that <u>angel</u> among them who saith "I am a god beside Him," will we recompense with hell: in such sort will we recompense the offenders.

Sura 21:100-112 - The angel shall meet them with, "This is your day which ye were promised"

21:100 Therein shall they groan; but nought therein shall they hear to comfort them.

21:101 But they for whom we have before ordained good things, shall be far away from it:

21:102 Its slightest sound they shall not hear: in what their souls longed for, they shall abide for ever:

21:103 The great terror shall not trouble them; and the <u>angel</u> shall meet them with, "This is your day which you were promised."

21:104 On that day we will roll up the heaven as one rolleth up written scrolls.

21:105 As we made the first creation, so will we bring it forth again. This promise bindeth us; verily, we will perform it.

21:106 And now, since the Law was given, have we written in the Psalms that "my servants, the righteous, shall inherit the earth."

21:107 Verily, in this Koran is teaching for those who serve God. We have not sent thee otherwise than as mercy unto all creatures.

21:108 Say: Verily it hath been revealed to me that your God is one God; are you then resigned to Him? (Muslims.)

21:109 But if they turn their backs, then say: I have warned you all alike; but I know not whether that with which you are threatened be nigh or distant.

21:110 God truly knoweth what is spoken aloud, and He also knoweth that which you hide.

21:111 And I know whether haply this delay be not for your trial, and that you may enjoy yourselves for a time.

21:112 My Lord saith: Judge you with truth; for our Lord is the God of Mercy - - whose help is to be sought against what you utter.

Sura 22 Al-Hajj (The Pilgramage)

Sura 22:70-79 - God chooseth messengers from among the angels and from among men

22:70 They worship beside God, that for which He hath sent down no warranty, and that of which they have no knowledge: but for those who commit this wrong, no helper!

22:71 And when our clear signs are rehearsed to them, thou mayst perceive disdain in the countenances of the Infidels. Scarce can they refrain from rushing to attack those who rehearse our signs to them!

22:72 Say: Shall I tell you of worse than this? The fire which God hath threatened to those who believer not! Wretched the passage thither!

22:73 O men! a parable is set forth to you, wherefore hearken to it. Verily, they on whom you call beside God, cannot create a fly, though they assemble for it; and if the fly carry off aught from them, they cannot take it away from it! Weak the suppliant and the supplicated!

22:74 Unworthy the estimate they form of God! for God is right Powerful, Mighty!

22:75 God chooseth messengers from among the <u>angels</u> and from among men: verily, God Heareth, Seeth.

22:76 He knoweth what is before them and what is behind them; and unto God shall all things return.

22:77 Believers! bow down and prostrate yourselves and worship your Lord, and work righteousness that you may fare well.

22:78 And do valiantly in the cause of God as it behoveth you to do for Him. He hath elected you, and hath not laid on you any hardship in religion, the Faith of your father Abraham. He hath named you the Muslims

22:79 Heretofore and in this Book, that the Apostles may be a witness against you, and that you may be witnesses against the rest of mankind. Therefore observe prayer, and pay the legal impost, and cleave fast to God. He is your liege Lord – a goodly Lord, and goodly Helper!

Sura 23 Al-Mu'minun (The Believers)

Sura 23:40-45 - The shout of the destroying angel in justice surprised them

23:40 This is merely a man who forgeth a lie about God: and we will not believe him."

23:41 He said, "O my Lord! help me against this charge of imposture."

23:42 He said, "yet a little, and they will soon repent them!" Then did the shout of the destroying <u>angel</u> injustice surprise them, and we made them like leaves swept down by a torrent,. Away then with the wicked people!

23:43 Then raised we up other generations after them –

23:44 Neither too soon, nor too late, shall a people reach its appointed time –

23:45 Then sent we our apostles one after another. Oft as their apostle presented himself to a nation, they treated him as a liar; and we caused one nation to follow another; and we made them the burden of a tale. Away then with the people who believe not!

Sura 23:100-118 - Recording angels

23:100 And I betake me to Thee, O my Lord! that they gain no hurtful access to me."

23:101 When death overtaketh one of the wicked, he saith, "Lord, send me back again,

23:102 That I may do the good which I have left undone." "By no means." These are the very words which he shall speak: But behind them shall be a barrier, until the day when they shall be raised again.

23:103 And when the trumpet shall be sounded, the ties of kindred between them shall cease on that day; neither shall they ask each other's help.

23:104 They whose balances shall be heavy, shall be the blest.

23:105 But they whose balances shall be light, – these are they who shall lose their souls, abiding in hell for ever:

23:106 The fire shall scorch their faces, and their lips shall quiver therein: –

23:107 "What! Were not my signs rehearsed unto you? and did you not treat them as lies?"

23:108 They shall say, "O our Lord! our ill-fortune prevailed against us, and we became an erring people.

23:109 O our Lord! Bring us forth hence: if we go back against to our signs, we shall indeed be evil doers."

23:110 He will say; "Be you driven down into it; and, address me not."

23:111 A part truly of my servants was there, who said, "O our Lord! we believe: forgive us, then, and be merciful to us, for of the merciful art thou the best."

23:112 But you received them with such scoffs that they suffered you to forget my warning, and you laughed them to scorn.

23:113 Verily this day will I reward them, for their patient endurance: the blissful ones shall they be!

23:114 He will say, "What number of years tarried you on earth?"

23:115 They will say, "We tarried a day, or part of a day; but ask the recording angels."

23:116 God will say, "Short indeed was the time you tarried, if that you knew it.

23:117 What! Did you then think that we had created you for pastime, and that you should not be brought back again to us?" Wherefore let God be exalted, the King, the Truth! There is no god but He! Lord of the stately throne! And whoso, together with God, shall call on another god, for whom he had no proof, shall surely have to give account to his Lord. Aye, it shall fare ill with the infidels.

23:118 And say: "O my Lord, pardon, and have mercy; for of those who show mercy, art thou the best."

Sura 25 Al-Furqun (The Criterion)

Sura 25:1-21 - An angel be sent down and take part in his warnings

25:1 Blessed be He who hath sent down Al Furkan (the illumination) on his servant, that to all creatures he may be a warner.

25:2 His the Kingdom of the Heavens and of the Earth! No son hath He begotten! No partner hath He in his Empire! All things hath He created, and decreeing hath decreed their destinies.

25:3 Yet have they adopted gods beside Him which have created nothing, but were themselves created:

25:4 And no power have they over themselves for evil or for good, nor have they power of death, or of life, or of raising the dead.

25:5 And the infidels say, "This Koran is a mere fraud of his own devising, and others have helped him with it, who had come hither by outrage and life."

25:6 And they say, "Tales of the ancients that he hath put in writing! and they were dictated to him morn and even."

25:7 Say: He hath sent it down who knoweth the secrets of the Heavens and of the Earth. He truly is the Gracious, the Merciful.

25:8 And they say, "What sort of apostle is this? He eateth food and he walketh the streets! Unless an <u>angel</u> be sent down and take part in his warnings,

25:9 Or a treasure be thrown down to him, or he have a garden that supplieth him with food..." and those unjust persons say, "You follow but a man enchanted."

25:10 See what likenesses they strike out for thee! But they err, and cannot find their way.

25:11 Blessed be He who if he please can give thee better than that of which they speak – Gardens, 'neath which the rivers flow: and pavilions will He assign thee.

25:12 Aye, they have treated the coming of "the Hour" as a lie. But a flaming fire have we got ready for those who treat the coming of the Hour as a lie.

25:13 When it shall see them from afar, they shall hear its raging and roaring, –

25:14 And when they shall be flung into a narrow space thereof bound together, they shall invoke destruction on the spot: - "Call not this day for one destruction, but call for destructions many."

25:15 Say: Is this, or the Paradise of Eternity which was promised to the

25:16 God-fearing, best? Their recompense shall it be and their retreat;

25:17 Abiding therein for ever, they shall have it in all that they desire! It is a promise to be claimed of thy Lord.

25:18 And on the day when he shall gather them together, and those whom they worshipped beside God, he will say, "Was it you who led these my servants astray, or of themselves strayed they from the path?"

25:19 They will say, "Glory be to thee! It beseemed not us to take other lords than thee. But thou gavest them and their fathers their fill of good things, till they forgat the remembrance of thee, and became a lost people."

25:20 Then will God say to the Idolaters, "Now have they made you liars in what you say, and they have no power to avert your doom, or to succour you."

25:21 And whosoever of you thus offendeth, we will make him taste a great punishment.

Sura 25:22-30 - If the angels be not sent down to us ... When they shall see the angels ... and the angels shall be sent down

25:22 Never have we sent Apostles before thee who ate not common food, and walked not the streets. And we test you by means of each other.

25:23 Will you be steadfast? Thy Lord is looking on!

25:24 They who look not forward to meet Us say, "If the angels be not sent down to us, or unless we behold our Lord...." Ah! they are proud of heart, and exceed with great excess!

25:25 On the day when they shall see the angels, no good news shall there be for the guilty ones, and they shall cry out, "A barrier than cannot be passed!"

25:26 Then will we proceed to the works which they have wrought, and make them as scattered dust.

25:27 Happier, on that day, the inmates of the Garden as to abode, and better off as to place of noontide slumber!

25:28 On that day shall the heaven with its clouds be cleft, and the angels shall be sent down, descending:

25:29 On that day shall all empire be in very deed with the God of Mercy, and hard day shall it be for the Infidels.

25:30 And on that day shall the wicked one bite his hands, and say, "Oh! would that I had taken the same path with the Apostle!

Sura 32 As-Sajdah (The Prostration)

Sura 32:5-11 - The angel of death who is charged with you shall cause you to die

32:5 This is He who knoweth the unseen and the seen; the Mighty, the Merciful,

32:6 Who hath made everything which he hath created most good; and began the creation of man with clay;

32:7 Then ordained his progeny from germs of life, from sorry water:

32:8 Then shaped him, and breathed of His Spirit into him, and gave you hearing and seeing and hearts: what little thanks do you return!

32:9 And they say, "What! when we shall have laid hidden in the earth, shall we become a new creation?"

32:10 Yea, they deny that they shall meet their Lord.

32:11 Say: The angel of death who is charged with you shall cause you to die: then shall you be returned to your Lord.

Sura 33 Al-Ahzab (The Clans)

Sura 33:40-46 - His angels intercede for you that He may bring you forth out of darkness into light

33:40 Muhammad is not the father of any man among you, but he is the Apostle of God, and the seal of the prophets: and God knoweth all things.

33:41 O Believers! remember God with frequent remembrance, and praise Him morning and evening.

33:42 He blesseth you, and His <u>angels</u> intercede for you, that He may bring you forth out of darkness into light: and Merciful is He to the Believers.

33:43 Their greeting on the day when they shall meet Him shall be "Peace!" And He hath got ready for them a noble recompense. O Prophet! we have sent thee to be a witness, and a herald of glad tidings, and a warner;

33:44 And one who, through His own permission, summoneth to god, and a light-giving torch.

33:45 Announce, therefore, to believers, that great boons do await them from God;

33:46 And obey not the Infidels and Hypocrites – yet abstain from injuring them: and put thou thy trust in God, for God is a sufficient guardian.

Sura 33:56 - God and His Angels bless the Prophet!

33:56 Verily, God and His <u>Angels</u> bless the Prophet! Bless you Him, O Believers, and salute Him with salutations of Peace.

Sura 34 Saba

Sura 34:39-41 - Asking the angels if his servants worshipped them

34:39 One day he will gather them all together: then shall he say to the angels, "Did these worship you?"

34:40 They shall say, "Glory be to thee! Thou art our master, not these! But they worshipped the Djinn: it was in them that most of them believed.

34:41 On this day the one of you shall have no power over others for help or hurt. And we will say to the evil doers, "Taste you the torment of the fire, which you treated as a delusion."

Sura 35 Al-Mala Ikah (The Angels)

Sura 35:1-2 - God employeth the angels as envoys

35:1 Praise be to God, Maker of the Heavens and of the Earth! Who employeth the angels as envoys, with pairs of wings, two, three and four: He addeth to his creature what He will! Truly God hath power for all things.

35:2 The mercy which God layeth open for man, no one can keep back; and what He shall keep back, none can afterwards send forth. And He is the Mighty, the Wise.

Sura 36 Ya Sin

Sura 36:10-31 - No sending down our angels but one shout from Gabriel and they were extinct

36:10 Him only shalt thou really warn, who followeth the monition and feareth the God of mercy in secret: him cheer with tidings of pardon, and of a noble recompense.

36:11 Verily, it is We who will quicken the dead, and write down the works which they have sent on before them, and the traces which they shall have left behind them: and everything have we set down in the clear Book of our decrees.

36:12 Set forth to them the instance of the people of the city when the Sent

36:13 Ones came to it.

36:14 When we sent two unto them and they charged them both with imposture – therefore with a third we strengthened them: and they said, "Verily we are the Sent unto you of God."

36:15 They said, "You are only men like us: Nought hath the God of Mercy sent down. You do nothing but lie."

36:16They said, "our Lord knoweth that we are surely sent unto you; To proclaim a clear message is our only duty."

36:17 They said, "Of a truth we augur ill from you: if you desist not we will surely stone you, and a grievous punishment will surely befall you from us."

36:18 They said, "Your augury of ill is with yourselves. Will you be warned? Nay, we are an erring people."

36:19 Then from the end of the city a man came running: He said, "O my people! follow the Sent Ones;

36:20 Follow those who ask not of you a recompense, and who are rightly guided.

36:21 And why should I not worship Him who made me, and to whom you shall be brought back?

36:22 Shall I take gods beside Him? If the God of Mercy be pleased to afflict me, their intercession will not avert from me aught, nor will they deliver:

36:23 Truly then should I be in a manifest error.

36:24 Verily, in your Lord have I believed; therefore hear me."

36:25 It was said to him, "Enter thou into Paradise:" And he said, "Oh that my people knew

36:26 How gracious God hath been to me, and that He hath made me one of His honoured ones."

36:27 But no army sent we down out of heaven after his death, nor were we then sending down our angels –

36:28 There was but one shout from Gabriel, and lo! they were extinct.

36:29 Oh! the misery that rests upon my servants! No apostle cometh to them but they laugh him to scorn.

36:30 See they not how many generations we have destroyed before them?

36:31 Not to false gods is it that they shall be brought back, But all, gathered together, shall be set before Us.

Sura 37 As-Saffat (Those Who Set The Ranks)

Sura 37:1-10 - The angels ranged in order for Songs of Praise

37:1 By the angels ranged in order for Songs of Praise,

37:2 And by those who repel demons,

37:3 And by those who recite the Koran for warning,

37:4 Truly your God is but one,

37:5 Lord of the Heavens and of the Earth, and of all that is between them, and Lord of the East.

37:6 We have adorned the lower heaven with the adornment of the stars.

37:7 They serve also as a guard against every rebellious Satan,

37:8 That they overhear not what passeth in the assembly on high, for they are darted at from every side,

37:9 Driven off and consigned to a lasting torment;

37:10 While, if one steal a word by stealth, a glistening flame pursueth him.

Sura 37:11-19 - The angels the stronger creation?

37:11 Ask the Meccans then, Are they, or the <u>angels</u> whom we have made, the stronger creation? Aye, of coarse clay have we created them.

37:12 But while thou marvellest they mock;

37:13 When they are warned, no warning do they take;

37:14 And when they see a sign, they fall to mocking,

37:15 And say, "This is no other than clear sorcery: What! when dead, and turned to dust and bones, shall we indeed be raised?

37:16 Our sires also of olden times?"

37:18 Say, Yes; and you shall be covered with disgrace.

37:19 For, one blast only, and lo! they shall gaze around them,

Sura 37:148-160 - Have we created the angels females?

37:148 And because they believed, we continued their enjoyments for a season.

37:149 Inquire then of the Meccans whether thy Lord hath daughters, and they, sons?

37:150 Have we created the <u>angels</u> females? and did they witness it?

37:151 Is it not a falsehood of their own devising, when they say,

37:152 "God hath begotten"? They are indeed liars.

37:153 Would he have preferred daughters to sons?

37:154 What reason have you for thus judging?

37:155 Will you not then receive this warning?

37:156 Have you a clear proof for them?

37:157 Produce your Book if you speak truth.

37:158 And they make him to be of kin with the Djinn: but the Djinn have long known that these idolaters shall be brought up before God.

37:159 Far be the glory of God from what they impute to him.

37:160 "His faithful servants do not thus. Moreover, you and what you worship Shall not stir up any against God,

Sura 38 Sad

Sura 38:71-82 - The Lord said to the angels about the making of man and the angels prostrated themselves, save Eblis

38:71 When thy Lord said to the <u>angels</u>, "I am about to make man of clay,

38:72 And when I have formed him and breathed my spirit into him, then worshipping fall down before him."

38:73 And the <u>angels</u> prostrated themselves, all of them with one accord,

38:74 Save Eblis. He swelled with pride, and became an unbeliever.

38:75 "O Eblis," said God, "what hindereth thee from prostrating thyself before him whom my hands have made?

38:76 Is it that thou are puffed up with pride? or art thou a being of lofty merit?"

38:77 He said, "I am more excellent than he; me hast thou created of fire: of clay hast thou created him."

38:78 He said: "Begone then hence: thou art accursed,

38:79 And lo! my ban shall be on thee till the day of the reckoning."

38:80 He said: "O my Lord! respite me till the day of Resurrection."

38:81 He said, "One then of the respited shalt thou be,

38:82 Till the day of the time appointed."

Sura 39 Az-Zumar (The Troops)

Sura 39:61-75 - Thou shalt see the Angels circling around the Throne with praises of their Lord

39:61 But God shall rescue those who fear him into their safe retreat: no ill shall touch them, neither shall they be put to grief.

39:62 God is the creator of all things, and of all things is He the guardian!

39:63 His the keys of the Heaven and of the Earth! and – who believe not in the signs of God – these! they shall perish!

39:64 Say: What! do you then bid me worship other than God, O you ignorant ones?

39:65 But now hath it been revealed to thee and to those who flourished before thee, – "Verily, if thou join partners with God, vain shall be all thy work, and thyself shalt be of those who perish.

39:66 Nay, rather worship God! and be of those who render thanks."

39:67 But they have not deemed of God as is He due; for on the resurrection day the whole Earth shall be but his handful, and in his right hand shall the Heavens be folded together. Praise be to Him! and high be He uplifted above the partners they join with Him!

39:68 And there shall be a blast on the trumpet, and all who are in the Heavens and all who are in the Earth shall expire, save those whom God shall vouchsafe to live. Then shall there be another blast on it, and lo! arising they shall gaze around them:

39:69 And the earth shall shine with the light of her lord, and the Book shall be set, and the prophets shall be brought up, and the witnesses; and judgment shall be given between them with equity; and none shall be wronged:

39:70 And every soul shall receive as it shall have wrought, for well knoweth He men's actions.

39:71 And by troops shall the unbelievers be driven towards Hell, until when they reach it, its gates shall be opened, and its keepers shall say to them, "Came not apostles from among yourselves to you, reciting to you the signs of the Lord, and warning you of the meeting with Him on this your day?" They shall say, "Yes." But just is the sentence of punishment on the unbelievers.

39:72 It shall be said to them, "Enter you the gates of Hell, therein to dwell for ever;" and wretched the abode of the arrogant!

39:73 But those who feared their Lord shall be driven on by troops to Paradise, until when they reach it, its gates shall be opened, and its keepers shall say to them, "All hail! virtuous have you been: enter therein, to abide herein for ever."

39:74 And they shall say, "Praise be to God, who hath made good to us His promise, and hath given to us the earth as our heritage, that we may dwell in Paradise wherever we please!" And goodly is the reward of those who travailed virtuously.

39:75 And thou shalt see the Angels circling around the Throne with praises of their Lord: and judgment shall be pronounced between them with equity: and it shall be said, "Glory be to God the Lord of the Worlds."

Sura 41 Fusilat (They Are Expounded)

Sura 41:10-13 - We furnished the lower heaven with lights and guardian angels ... He had surely sent down angels

41:10 Then He applied himself to the Heaven, which then was but smoke: and to it and to the Earth He said, "Come you, whether in obedience or against your will?" and they both said, "We come obedient."

41:11 And He made them seven heavens in two days, and in each heaven made known its office: And we furnished the lower heaven with lights and guardian angels. This, the disposition of the Almighty, the Allknowing.

41:12 If they turn away, then say: I warn you of a tempest, like the tempest of Ad and Themoud!

41:13 When the apostles came to them, on every side, saying, "Worship none but God," they said, "Had our Lord been pleased to send down, He had surely sent down <u>angels</u>; and in sooth, your message we do not believe."

Sura 41:30-31 - The angels shall descend to them and say, "Fear ye not"

41:30 But as for those who say, "Our Lord is God;" and who go straight to Him, the <u>angels</u> shall descend to them and say, "Fear you not, neither be you grieved, but rejoice you in the paradise which you have been promised.

41:31 We are your guardians in this life and in the next: your's therein shall be your soul's desire, and your's therein whatever you shall ask for, The hospitality of a Gracious, a Merciful One."

Sura 42 Ash-Shura (Counsel)

Sura 42:2-4 - The angels celebrate the praise of their Lord

42:2 All that is in the Heavens and all that is in the Earth is His: and He is the High, the Great!

42:3 Ready are the Heavens to cleave asunder from above for very awe: and the <u>angels</u> celebrate the praise of their Lord, and ask forgiveness for the dwellers on earth: Is not God the Indulgent, the Merciful?

42:4 But whoso take aught beside Him as lords – God watcheth them! but thou hast them not in thy charge.

Sura 43 Az-Zukhruf (Ornaments of Gold)

Sura 43:10-20 - They make the angels who are the servants of God of Mercy, females

43:10 And who sendeth down out of Heaven the rain in due degree, by which we quicken a dead land; thus shall you be brought forth from the grave:

43:11 And who hath created the sexual couples, all of them, and hath made for you the ships and beasts whereon you ride:

43:12 That you may sit balanced on their backs and remember the goodness of your Lord as you sit so evenly therein, and say: "Glory to Him who hath subjected these to us! We could not have attained to it of ourselves:

43:13 And truly unto our Lord shall we return."

43:14 You do they assign to him some of his own servants for offspring!

43:15 Verily man is an open ingrate!

43:16 Hath God adopted daughters from among those whom he hath created, and chosen sons for you?

43:17 But when that is announced to any one of them, which he affirmeth to be the case with the God of Mercy, his face settleth into darkness and he is silent-sad.

43:18 What! make they a being to be the offspring of God who is brought up among trinkets, and is every contentious without reason?

43:19 And they make the angels who are the servants of God of Mercy, females. What! did they witness their creation? Their witness shall be taken down, and they shall hereafter be enquired at.

43:20 And they say: "Had the God of Mercy so willed it we should never have worshipped them." No knowledge have they in this: they only lie.

Sura 43:50-58 - A train of angels come with him

43:50 And Pharaoh made proclamation among his people. Said he, "O my people! is not the kingdom of Egypt mine, and these rivers which flow at my feet? Do you not behold?

43:51 Am I not mightier than this despicable fellow,

43:52 And who scarce can speak distinctly?

43:53 Have bracelets of gold then been put upon him, or come there with him a train of Angels?"

43:54 And he inspired his people with levity, and they obeyed him; for they were a perverse people:

43:55 And when they had angered us, we took vengeance on them, and we drowned them all.

43:56 And we made them a precedent and instance of divine judgments to those who came after them.

43:57 And when the Son of Mary was set forth as an instance of divine power, lo! thy people cried out for joy thereat:

43:58 And they said, "Are our gods or is he the better?" They put this forth to thee only in the spirit of dispute. Yea, they are a contentious people.

Sura 43:59-64 - ... (we could from yourselves bring forth Angels to succeed you on earth)

43:59 Jesus is no more than a servant whom we favoured, and proposed as an instance of divine power to the children of Israel.

43:60 (And if we pleased, we could from yourselves bring forth Angels to succeed you on earth:)

43:61 And he shall be a sign of the last hour; doubt not then of it, and follow you me: this is the right way;

43:62 And let not Satan turn you aside from it, for he is your manifest foe.

43:63 And when Jesus came with manifest proofs, he said, "Now am I come to you with wisdom; and a part of those things about which you are at variance I will clear up to you; fear you God therefore and obey me.

43:64 Verily, God is my Lord and your Lord; wherefore worship you him: this is a right way."

Sura 43:80-84 - Our angels are at their sides writing down secrets and private talks

43:80 Think they that we hear not their secrets and their private talk? yes, and our <u>angels</u> who are at their sides write them down.

43:81 Say: If the God of Mercy had a son, the first would I be to worship him:

43:82 But far be the Lord of the Heavens and of the Earth, the Lord of the Throne, from that which they impute to Him!

43:83 Wherefore let them alone, to plunge on, and sport, until they meet the day with which they are menaced.

43:84 He who is God in the Heavens is God in earth also: and He is the Wise, the Knowing.

Sura 47 Mohammad

Sura 47:27-32 - The angels shall smite them on the face and back

47:27 But as to those who return to their errors after "the guidance" hath been made plain to them, Satan shall beguile them, and fill them with his suggestions.

47:28 This – because they say to those who abhor what God hath sent down, "We will comply with you in part of what you enjoin." But God knoweth their secret reservations.

47:29 But how? When the <u>angels</u>, in causing them to die, shall smite them on the face and back!

47:30 This – because they follow that which angerth God, and abhor what pleaseth Him: therefore will He make their works fruitless.

47:31 Think these men of diseased hearts, that God will not bring out their malice to light?

47:32 If such were our pleasure, we could point them out to thee, and thou surely know them by their tokens: and know them thou shalt, by the strangeness of their words. God knoweth your doings.

Sura 50 Qaf

Sura 50:14-19 - Two angels; one sitting on the right hand and the other on the left

50:14 "Are we wearied out with the first creation? Yet are they in doubt with regard to a new creations!

50:15 We created man: and we know what his soul whispereth to him, and we are closer to him than his neck-vein.

50:16 When the two <u>angels</u> charged with taking account shall take it, one sitting on the right hand, the other of the left:

50:17 Not a word doth he utter, but there is a watcher with him ready to note it down:

50:18 And the stupor of certain death cometh upon him: - "This is what thou wouldst have shunned"—

50:19 And there shall be a blast on the trumpet, – it is the threatened day!

Sura 50:20-21 - Every soul shall come, and an angel with it urging it along and an angel to witness against it

50:20 And every soul shall come, – an <u>angel</u> with it urging it along, and an <u>angel</u> to witness against it –

50:21 saith he, "Of this day didst thou live in heedlessness: but we have taken off thy veil from thee, and thy sight is becoming sharp this day."

Sura 52 Al-Tur (The Mountain)

Sura 52:31-49 - Have they a ladder for hearing the angels?

52:31 Will they say, "A poet! let us await some adverse turn of his fortune?"

52:32 Say, wait you, and in sooth I too will wait with you.

52:33 Is it their dreams which inspire them with then? or is it that they are a perverse people?

52:34 Will they say, "He hath forged it (the Koran) himself?" Nay, rather it is that they believed not.

52:35 Let them then produce a discourse like it, if they speak the Truth.

52:36 Were they created by nothing? or were they the creators of themselves?

52:37 Created they the Heavens and the Earth? Nay, rather, they have no faith.

52:58 Hold they thy Lord's treasures? Bear they the rule supreme?

52:59 Have they a ladder for hearing the angels? Let any one who hath heard them bring a clear proof of it.

52:40 Asked thou pay of them? they are themselves weighed down with debts.

52:41 Have they such a knowledge of the secret things that they can write them down?

52:42 Desire they to lay snares for thee? But the snared ones shall be they who do not believe.

52:43 Have they any God beside God? Glory be to God above what they join with Him.

52:44 And should they see a fragment of the heaven falling down, they would say, "It is only a dense cloud."

52:45 Leave them then until they come face to face with the day when they shall swoon away:

52:46 A day in which their snares shall not at all avail them, neither shall they be helped.

52:47 And verily, beside this is there a punishment for the evil-doers: but most of them know it not.

52:48 Wait thou patiently the judgment of thy Lord, for thou art in our eye; and celebrate the praise of thy Lord when thou risest up,

52:49 And in the night-season: Praise him when the stars are setting.

Sura 53 An-Najm (The Star)

Sura 53:24-27 - Many as are the Angels in the Heavens, their intercession shall be of no avail

53:24 Shall man have whatever he wisheth?

53:25 The future and the present are in the hand of God:

53:26 And many as our the Angels in the Heavens, their intercession shall be of no avail

53:27 Until God hath permitted it to whom he shall please and will accept.

Sura 53:28-31 - Who name the angels with names of females

53:28 Verily, it is they who believe not in the life to come, who name the angels with names of females:

53:29 But herein they have no knowledge: they follow a mere conceit: and mere conceit can never take the place of truth.

53:30 Withdraw then from him who turneth his back on our warning and desireth only this present life.

53:31 This is the sum of their knowledge. Truly thy Lord best knoweth him who erreth from his way, and He best knoweth him who hath received guidance.

Sura 57 Al-Hadid (Iron)

Sura 57:10-14 - The angels shall say to them, "Good tidings for you this day ..."

57:10 And what hath come to you that you expend not for the cause of God? since the heritage of the Heavens and of the Earth is God's only! Those among you who contributed before the victory, and fought, shall be differently treated from certain others among you!

57:11 Such shall have a nobler grade than those who contributed and fought after it. But a goodly recompense hath God promised to all; and God is fully informed of your actions.

57:12 Who is he that will lend a generous loan to God? So will He double it to him, and he shall have a noble reward.

57:13 One day thou shalt see the believers, men and women, with their light running before them, and on their right hand. The angels shall say to them, "Good tidings for you this day of gardens beneath whose shades the rivers flow, in which you shall abide for ever!" This the great bliss!

57:14 On that day the hypocrites, both men and women, shall say to those who believe, "Tarry for us, that we may kindle our light at yours." It shall be said, "Return you back, and seek light for yourselves." But between them shall be set a wall with a gateway, within which shall be the Mercy, and in front, without it, the Torment. They shall cry to them, "Were we not with you?" They shall say, "Yes! but you led yourselves into temptation, and you delayed, and you doubted, and the good things you craved deceived you, till the doom of God arrived: – and the deceiver deceived you in regard to God."

Sura 66 At-Tahrim (Banning)

Sura 66:1-4 - Then know that God is the Prophet's protector, and Gabriel, and every just man among the faithful; and the angels are his helpers besides

66:1 Why, O Prophet! dost thou hold that to be forbidden which God hath made lawful to thee, from a desire to please thy wives, since God is Lenient, Merciful?

66:2 God hath allowed you release from your oaths; and God is your master: and He is the Knowing, the Wise.

66:3 When the prophet told a recent occurrence as a secret to one of his wives, and when she divulged it and God informed him of this, he acquainted her with part and withheld part. And when he had told her of it, she said, "Who told thee this?" He said, "The Knowing, the Sage hath told it me.

66:4 "If you both be turned to God in penitence, for now have your hearts gone astray.... but if you conspire against the Prophet, then know that God is his Protector, and Gabriel, and every just man among the faithful; and the angels are his helpers besides.

Sura 66:5-6 - Angels fierce and mighty are set over men

66:5 "Haply if he put you both away, his Lord will give him in exchange other wives better than you, Muslims, believers, devout, penitent, obedient, observant of fasting, both known of men and virgins."

66:6 O Believers! save yourselves and your families from the fire whose fuel is men and stones, over which are set angels fierce and mighty: they disobey not God in what He hath commanded them, but execute His behests.

Sura 69 Al-Haqqah (The Reality)

Sura 69:11-37 - The angels shall be on heaven's sides and over them that day eight shall bear up the throne of thy Lord

69:11 When the Flood rose high, we bare you in the Ark,

69:12 That we might make that event a warning to you, and that the retaining ear might retain it.

69:13 But when one blast shall be blown on the trumpet,

69:14 And the earth and the mountains shall be upheaved, and shall both be crushed into dust at a single crushing,

69:15 On that day the woe that must come suddenly shall suddenly come,

69:16 And the heaven shall cleave asunder, for on that day it shall be fragile;

69:17 And the angels shall be on its sides, and over them on that day eight shall bear up the throne of thy Lord.

69:18 On that day you shall be brought before Him: none of your hidden deeds shall remain hidden:

69:19 And he who shall have his book given to him in his right hand, will say to his friend, "Take you it; read you my book;

69:20 I ever thought that to this my reckoning I should come."

69:21 And his shall be a life that shall please him well,

69:22 In a lofty garden,

69:23 Whose clusters shall be near at hand:

69:24 "Eat you and drink with healthy relish, as the meed of what you sent on beforehand in the days which are past."

69:25 But he who shall have his book given into his left hand, will say, "O that my book had never been given me!

69:26 And that I had never known by reckoning!

69:27 O that death had made an end of me!

69:28 My wealth hath not profited me!

69:29My power hath perished from me!"

69:30 "Lay you hold on him and chain him,

69:31 Then at the Hell-fire burn him,

69:32 Then into a chain whose length is seventy cubits thrust him

69:33 For he believed not in God, the Great,

69:34 And was not careful to feed the poor;

69:35 No friend therefore shall he have here this day,

69:36 Nor food, but corrupt sores,

69:37 Which none shall eat but the sinners."

Sura 70 Al-Maarif (The Ascending Stairways)

Sura 70:1-28 - The angels and the spirit ascend to him in a day, whose length is fifty thousand years

70:1 A suitor sued for punishment to light suddenly

70:2 On the infidels: None can hinder

70:3 God from inflicting it, the master of those Ascents,

70:4 By which the angels and the spirit ascend to him in a day, whose length is fifty thousand years.

70:5 Be thou patient therefore with becoming patience;

70:6 They forsooth regard that day as distant,

70:7 But we see it nigh:

70:8 The day when the heavens shall become as molten brass,

70:9 And the mountains shall become like flocks of wool:

70:10 And friend shall not question of friend,

70:11 Though they look at one another. Fain would the wicked redeem himself from punishment on that day at the price of his children,

70:12 Of his spouse and his brother,

70:13 And of his kindred who shewed affection for him,

70:14 And of all who are on the earth that then it might deliver him.

70:15 But no. For the fire,

70:16 Dragging by the scalp,

70:17 Shall claim him who turned his back and went away,

70:18 And amassed and hoarded.

70:19 Man truly is by creation hasty;

70:20 When evil befalleth him, impatient;

70:21 But when good falleth to his lot, tenacious.

70:22 No so the prayerful,

70:23 Who are ever constant at their prayers;

70:24 And of whose substance there is a due and stated portion

70:25 For him who asketh, and for him who is ashamed to beg;

70:26 And who own the judgment-day a truth,

70:27 And who thrill with dread at the chastisement of their Lord –

70:28 For there is none safe from the chastisement of their Lord –

Sura 74 Al-Mudath-this (The Cloaked One)

Sura 74:10-35 - Over Hell-fire is nineteen angels and none but angels have we made guardians of the fire

74:10 A day, to the Infidels, devoid of ease.

74:11 Leave me alone to deal with him whom I have created,

74:12 And on whom I have bestowed vast riches,

74:13 And sons dwelling before him,

74:14 And for whom I have smoothed all things smoothly down; –

74:15 Yet desireth he that I shall add more!

74:16 But no! because to our signs he is a foe

74:17 I will lay grievous woes upon him.

74:18 For he plotted and he planned!

74:19 May he be cursed! How he planned!

74:20 Again, may be be cursed! How he planned!

74:21 Then looked he around him,

74:22 Then frowned and scowled,

74:23 Then turned his back and swelled with disdain,

74:24 And said, "This is merely magic that will be wrought;

74:25 It is merely the word of a mortal."

74:26 We will surely cast him in Hell-fire.

74:27 And who shall teach thee what Hell-fire is?

74:28 It leaveth nought, it spareth nought,

74:29 Blackening the skin.

74:30 Over it are nineteen angels.

74:31 None but angels have we made guardians of the fire: nor have we made this to be their number but to perplex the unbelievers, and that they who possess the Scriptures may be certain of the truth of the

74:32 Koran, and that they who believe may increase their faith;

74:33 And that they to whom the Scriptures have been given, and the believers,may not doubt;

74:34 And that the infirm of heart and the unbelievers may say, What meaneth God by this parable?

74:35 Thus God misleadeth whom He will, and whom He will doth He guide aright: and none knoweth the armies of thy Lord but Himself: and this is no other than a warning to mankind.

Sura 78 An-Naba (The Tidings)

Sura 78:30-40 - The Spirit and the Angels shall be ranked in order

78:30 "Taste this then: and we will give you increase of nought but torment."

78:31 But, for the God-fearing is a blissful abode,

78:32 Enclosed gardens and vineyards;

78:33 And damsels with swelling breasts, their peers in age,

78:34 And a full cup:

78:35 There shall they hear no vain discourse nor any falsehood:

78:36 A recompense from thy Lord – sufficing gift! –

78:37 Lord of the heavens and of the earth, and of all that between them lieth - the God of Mercy! But not a word shall they obtain from Him.

78:38 On the day whereon the Spirit and the Angels shall be ranked in order, they shall not speak: save he whom the God of Mercy shall permit, and who shall say that which is right.

78:39 This is the sure day. Whoso then will, let him take the path of return to his Lord.

78:40 Verily, we warn you of a chastisement close at hand: The day on which a man shall see the deeds which his hands have sent before him; and when the unbeliever shall say, "Oh! would I were dust!"

Sura 79 An-Naziat (Those Who Dragged Forth)

Sura 79:1-9 - Those angels who drag forth souls with violence

79:1 By those <u>angels</u> who drag forth souls with violence,

79:2 And by those who with joyous release release them;

79:3 By those who swim swimmingly along;

79:4 By those who are foremost with foremost speed;

79:5 By those who conduct the affairs of the universe!

79:6 One day, the disturbing trumpet-blast shall disturb it,

79:7 Which the second blast shall follow:

79:8 Men's hearts on that day shall quake: –

79:9 Their looks be downcast.

Sura 81 - At-Takwir (The Overthrowing)

Sura 81:10-28 - The Lord of the Throne is obeyed there by Angels, faithful to his trust

81:10 And when the leaves of the Book shall be unrolled,

81:11 And when the Heavens shall be stripped away,

81:12 And when Hell shall be made to blaze,

81:13 And when Paradise shall be brought near,

81:14 Every soul shall know what it hath produced.

81:15 It needs not that I swear by the stars of retrograde motions Which move swiftly and hide themselves away,

81:16 And by the night when it cometh darkening on,

81:17 And by the dawn when it brighteneth,

81:18 That this is the word of an illustrious Messenger,

81:19 Endued with power, having influence with the Lord of the Throne,

81:20 Obeyed there by <u>Angels</u>, faithful to his trust,

81:21 And your compatriot is not one possessed by djinn;

81:23 For he saw him in the clear horizon:

81:24 Nor doth he teach the doctrine of a cursed Satan.

81:25 Whither then are you going?

81:26 Verily, this is no other than a warning to all creatures;

81:27 To him among you who willeth to walk in a straight path:

81:28 But will it you shall not, unless as God willeth it, the Lord of the worlds.

Sura 83 At-Tatfif (Defrauding)

Sura 83:10-36 - The angels who draw nigh unto God attest

83:10 Woe, on that day, to those who treated our signs as lies,

83:11 Who treated the day of judgment as a lie!

83:12 None treat it as a lie, save the transgressor, the criminal,

83:14 Who, when our signs are rehearsed to him, saith, "Tales of the Ancients!"

83:15 Yes; but their own works have got the mastery over their hearts.

83:16 Yes; they shall be shut out as by a veil from their Lord on that day; Then shall they be burned in Hell-fire:

83:17 Then shall it be said to them, "This is what you deemed a lie."

83:18 Even so. But the register of the righteous is in Illiyoun.

83:19 And who shall make thee understand what Illiyoun is?

83:20 A book distinctly written;

83:21 The <u>angels</u> who draw nigh unto God attest it.

83:22 Surely, among delights shall the righteous dwell!

83:23 Seated on bridal couches they will gaze around;

83:24 Thou shalt mark in their faces the brightness of delight;

83:25 Choice sealed wine shall be given them to quaff,

83:26 The seal of musk. For this let those pant who pant for bliss –

83:27 Mingled therewith shall be the waters of Tasnim –

83:28 Fount whereof they who draw nigh to God shall drink.

83:29 The sinners indeed laugh the faithful to scorn:

83:30 And when they pass by them they wink at one another, –

83:31 And when they return to their own people, they return jesting,

83:32 And when they see them they say, "These are the erring ones."

83:33 And yet they have no mission to be their guardians.

83:34 Therefore, on that day the faithful shall laugh the infidels to scorn,

83:35 As reclining on bridal couches they behold them.

83:36 Shall not the infidels be recompensed according to their works?

Sura 89 Al-Fajr (The Dawn)

Sura 89:12-30 - The angels rank on rank shall come with the Lord

89:12 Wherefore thy Lord let loose on them the scourge of chastisement,

89:13 For thy Lord standeth on a watch tower.

89:14 As to man, when his Lord trieth him and honoureth him and is bounteous to him,

89:15 Then saith he, "My Lord honoureth me:"

89:16 But when he proveth him and limiteth his gifts to him,

89:17 He saith, "My Lord despiseth me."

89:18 Aye. But you honour not the orphan,

89:19 Nor urge you one another to feed the poor,

89:20 And you devour heritages, devouring greedily,

89:21 And you love riches with exceeding love.

89:22 Aye. But when the earth shall be crushed with crushing, crushing,

89:23 And thy Lord shall come and the angels rank on rank,

89:24 And Hell on that day shall be moved up, – Man shall on that day remember himself. But how shall remembrance help him?

89:25 He shall say, Oh! would that I had prepared for this my life! On that day none shall punish as God punisheth,

89:26 And none shall bind with such bonds as He.

89:27 Oh, thou soul which art at rest,

89:28 Return to thy Lord, pleased, and pleasing him:

89:29Enter thou among my servants,

89:30 And enter thou my Paradise.

Sura 96 Al-Alaq (The Clot)

Sura 96:27-34 - Nineteen angels are over the Hell-fire and none but angels have we made guardians of the fire

96:27 "And who shall teach thee what Hell-fire is?

96:28 It leaveth nought, it spareth nought,

96:29 Blackening the skin.

96:30 Over it are nineteen angels.

96:31 None but <u>angels</u> have we made guardians of the fire: nor have we made this to be their number but to perplex the unbelievers, and that they who possess the Scriptures may be certain of the truth of the Korna, and that they who believe may increase their faith;

96:32 And that they to whom the Scriptures have been given, and the believers, may not doubt;

96:33 And that the infirm of heart and the unbelievers may say, What meaneth God by this parable?

96:34 Thus God misleadeth whom He will, and whom He will doth He guide aright: and none knoweth the armies of they Lord but Himself: and this is no other than a warning to mankind."

Sura 97 Al-Qadr (Power)

Sura 97:1-5 - The angels descend on the night of power

97:1 Verily, we have caused It to descend on the night of Power.

97:2 And who shall teach thee what the night of power is?

97:3 The night of power excelleth a thousand months:

97:4 Therein descend the <u>angels</u> and the spirit by permission of their Lord for every matter;

97:5 And all is peace till the breaking of the morn.

GABRIEL

Sura 2

Sura 2:90-94 - Whoso is the enemy of Gabriel, angels, and Michael shall have God as his enemy

2:90 And thou wilt surely find them of all men most covetous of life, beyond even the polytheists. To be kept alive a thousand years might one of them desire: but that he may be preserved alive, shall no one reprieve himself from the punishment! And God seeth what they do.

2:91 Say: Whoso is the enemy of <u>Gabriel</u> – For he it is who by God's leave hath caused the Koran to descend on thy heart, the confirmation of previous revelations, and guidance, and good tidings to the faithful –

2:92 Whoso is an enemy to God or his <u>angels,</u> or to <u>Gabriel,</u> or to <u>Michael,</u> shall have God as his enemy: for verily God is an enemy to the Infidels.

2:93 Moreover, clear signs have we sent down to thee, and one will disbelieve them but the perverse.

2:94 Oft as they have formed an engagement with thee, will some of them set it aside? But most of them believe not.

Sura 29

Sura 29:30-43 - Gabriel's terrible cry of surprise

29:30 And when our messengers came to Abraham with the tidings of a son, they said, "Of a truth we will destroy in in-dwellers in this city, for its in-dwellers are evil doers."

29:31 He said, "Lot is therein." They said, "We know full well who therein is.

29:32 Him and his family will we save, except his wife; she will be of those who linger.

29:33 And when our messengers came to Lot, he was troubled for them, and his arm was too weak to protect them; and they said, "Fear not, and distress not thyself, for thee and thy family will we save, except thy wife; she will be of those who linger.

29:34 We will surely bring down upon the dwellers in this city vengeance from Heaven for the excesses they have committed."

29:35 And in what we have left of it is a clear sign to men of understanding.

29:36 And to Madian we sent their brother Shoaib. And he said, "Oh! my people! worship God, and expect the latter day, and enact not in the land deeds of harmful excess."

29:37 But they treated him as an imposter: so an earthquake assailed them; and at morn they were found prostrate and dead in their dwellings.

29:38 And we destroyed Ad and Themoud. Already is this made plain to you in the ruins of their dwellings. For Satan had made their own works fair seeming to them, and drew them from the right path, keensighted though they were.

29:39 And Corah and Pharaoh and Haman. With proofs of his mission did Moses come to them, and they behaved proudly on the earth; but us they could not outstrip; For, every one of them did we seize in his sin. Against some of them did we sent a stone-charged wind: Some of them did the terrible cry of <u>Gabriel</u> surprise: for some of them we cleaved the earth; and some of them we drowned. And it was not God who would deal wrongly by them, but they wronged themselves.

29:40 The likeness for those who take to themselves guardians instead of God is the likeness of the spider who buildeth her a house: But verily, frailest of all houses surely is the house of the spider. Did they but know this!

29:41 God truly knoweth all that they call on beside Him; and He is the Mighty, the Wise.

29:42 These similitudes do we set forth to men: and one understand them except the wise.

29:43 God hath created the Heavens and the Earth for a serious end. Verily in this is a sign to those who believe.

Sura 36

Sura 36:20-32 - One shout from Gabriel and they were extinct

36:20 Follow those who ask not of you a recompense, and who are rightly guided.

36:21 And why should I not worship Him who made me, and to whom you shall be brought back?

36:22 Shall I take gods beside Him? If the God of Mercy be pleased to afflict me, their intercession will not avert from me aught, nor will they deliver:

36:23 Truly then should I be in a manifest error.

36:24 Verily, in your Lord have I believed; therefore hear me."

36:25 - It was said to him, "Enter thou into Paradise:" And he said, "Oh that my people knew

36:26 How gracious God hath been to me, and that He hath made me one of His honoured ones."

36:27 But no army sent we down out of heaven after his death, nor were we then sending down our angels –

36:28 There was but one shout from Gabriel, and lo! they were extinct.

36:29 Oh! the misery that rests upon my servants! No apostle cometh to them but they laugh him to scorn.

36:30 See they not how many generations we have destroyed before them?

36:31 Not to false gods is it that they shall be brought back,

36:32 But all, gathered together, shall be set before Us.

Sura 42

Sura 42:48-53 - We sent the Spirit (Gabriel) to thee with a revelation, by our command - (The Book of Koran)

42:48 God's, the kingdom of the Heavens and of the Earth! He createth what He will! and he giveth daughters to whom He will, and sons to whom He will:

42:49 Or He giveth them children of both sexes, and He maketh whom He will to be childless; for He is Wise, Powerful!

42:50 It is not for man that God should speak with him but by vision, or from behind a veil:

42:51 Or, He sendeth a messenger to reveal, by his permission, what He will: for He is Exalted, Wise!

42:52 Thus have we sent the Spirit (Gabriel) to thee with a revelation, by our command. Thou knowest not, ere this, what "the Book" was, or what the faith. But we have ordained it for a light: by it will we guide whom we please of our servants. And thou shalt surely guide into the right way,

42:53 The way of God, whose is all that the Heaven and the Earth contain.

Sura 53

Sura 53:1-28 - Gabriel is implied as the One terrible in Power who taught it him

53:1 By the star when it setteth,

53:2 Your compatriot erreth not, nor is he led astray,

53:3 Neither speaketh he from mere impulse.

53:4 The Koran is no other than a revelation revealed to him:

53:5 One terrible in power taught it him,

53:6 Endued with wisdom. With even balance stood he

53:7 In the highest part of the horizon:

53:8 Then came he nearer and approached,

53:9 And was at the distance of two bows, or even closer, –

53:10 And he revealed to his servant what he revealed.

53:11 His heart falsified not what he saw.

53:12 What! will you then dispute with him as to what he saw?

53:13 He had seen him also another time,

53:14 Near the Sidra-tree, which marks the boundary.

53:15 Near which is the garden of respose.

53:16 When the Sidrah-tree was covered with what covered it,

53:17 His eye turned not aside, nor did it warner:

53:18 For he saw the greatest of the signs of his Lord.

53:19 Do you see At-Lat and Al-Ozza,

53:20 And Manat the third idol besides?

53:21 What? shall you have male progeny and God female?

53:22 This were indeed an unfair partition!

53:23 These are mere names: you and your fathers named them thus: God hath not sent down any warranty in their regard. A mere conceit and their own impulses do they follow. Yet hath "the guidance" from their

53:24 Lord come to them.

53:25 Shall man have whatever he wisheth?

53:26 The future and the present are in the hand of God:

53:27 And many as our the Angels in the Heavens, their intercession shall be of no avail

53:28 Until God hath permitted it to whom he shall please and will accept.

Sura 66

Sura 66:1-6 - Then know that God is the Prophet's protector, and Gabriel, and every just man among the faithful; and the angels are his helpers besides - angels fierce and mighty are set over men and stones

66:1 Why, O Prophet! dost thou hold that to be forbidden which God hath made lawful to thee, from a desire to please thy wives, since God is Lenient, Merciful?

66:2 God hath allowed you release from your oaths; and God is your master: and He is the Knowing, the Wise.

66:3 When the prophet told a recent occurrence as a secret to one of his wives, and when she divulged it and God informed him of this, he acquainted her with part and withheld part. And when he had told her of it, she said, "Who told thee this?" He said, "The Knowing, the Sage hath told it me.

66:4 "If you both be turned to God in penitence, for now have your hearts gone astray.... but if you conspire against the Prophet, then know that God is his Protector, and Gabriel, and every just man among the faithful; and the angels are his helpers besides.

66:5 "Haply if he put you both away, his Lord will give him in exchange other wives better than you, Muslims, believers, devout, penitent, obedient, observant of fasting, both known of men and virgins."

66:6 O Believers! save yourselves and your families from the fire whose fuel is men and stones, over which are set angels fierce and mighty: they disobey not God in what He hath commanded them, but execute His behests.

Sura 81

Sura 81:10-28 - Gabriel is implied as an illustrious Messenger bringing the word and obeyed by Angels

81:10 And when the leaves of the Book shall be unrolled,

81:11 And when the Heavens shall be stripped away,

81:12 And when Hell shall be made to blaze,

81:13 And when Paradise shall be brought near,

81:14 Every soul shall know what it hath produced.

81:15 It needs not that I swear by the stars of retrograde motions

81:16 Which move swiftly and hide themselves away,

82:17 And by the night when it cometh darkening on,

82:18 And by the dawn when it brighteneth,

82:19 That this is the word of an illustrious Messenger,

81:20 Endued with power, having influence with the Lord of the Throne,

81:21 Obeyed there by Angels, faithful to his trust,

81:22 And your compatriot is not one possessed by djinn;

81:23 For he saw him in the clear horizon:

81:24 Nor doth he teach the doctrine of a cursed Satan.

81:25 Whither then are you going?

81:26 Verily, this is no other than a warning to all creatures;

81:27 To him among you who willeth to walk in a straight path:

81:28 But will it you shall not, unless as God willeth it, the Lord of the worlds.

GABRIEL AS SPIRIT

Sura 16

Sura 16:100-107 - Holy Spirit hath brought it down with the truth from the Lord

16:100 When thou readest the Koran, have recourse to God for help against Satan the stoned,

16:101 For no power hath he over those who believe, and put their trust in their Lord,

16:102 But only hath he power over those who turn away from God, and join other deities with Him.

16:103 And when we change one (sign) verse for another, and God knoweth best what He revealeth, they say, "Thou art only a fabricator." Nay! but most of them have no knowledge.

16:104 Say: The Holy Spirit hath brought it down with truth from thy Lord, that

16:105 He may stablish those who have believed, and as guidance and glad tidings to the Muslims.

16:106 We also know that they say, "Surely a certain person teacheth him."

16:107 But the tongue of him at whom they hint is foreign, while this Koran is in the plain Arabic.

Sura 19

Sura 19:1-24 - We sent our spirit to her - I am only a messenger of thy Lord

19:1 Kaf. Ha. Ya. Ain. Sad. A recital of thy Lord's mercy to his servant Zachariah;

19:2 When he called upon his Lord with secret calling,

19:3 And said, "O Lord, verily my bones are weakened, and the hoar hairs glisten on my head,

19:4 And never, Lord, have I prayed to thee with ill success.

19:5 But now I have fears for my kindred after me; and my wife is barren:

19:6 Give me, then, a successor as thy special gift, who shall be my heir and an heir of the family of Jacob: and make him, Lord, well pleasing to thee."

19:7 - "O Zachariah! verily we announce to thee a son, – his name John:

19:8 That name We have given to none before him."

19:9 He said: "O my Lord! how when my wife is barren shall I have a son, and when I have now reached old age, failing in my powers?"

19:10 He said: So shall it be. Thy Lord hath said, Easy is this to me, for I created thee aforetime when thou wast nothing."

19:11 He said, "Vouchsafe me, O my Lord! a sign." He said: "Thy sign shall be that for three nights, though sound in health, thou speakest not to man."

19:12 And he came forth from the sanctuary to his people, and made signs to them to sign praises morn and even.

19:13 We said: "O John! receive the Book with purpose of heart:" – and

19:14 We bestowed on him wisdom while yet a child;

19:15 And mercifulness from Ourself, and purity; and pious was he, and duteous to his parents; and not proud, rebellious.

19:16 And peace was on him on the day he was born, and the day of his death, and shall be on the day when he shall be raised to life!

19:17 And make mention in the Book, of Mary, when she went apart from her family, eastward, And took a veil to shroud herself from them: and we sent our spirit to her, and he took before her the form of a perfect man.

19:18 She said: "I fly for refuge from thee to the God of Merch! If thou fearest Him, begone from me."

19:19 He said: "I am only a <u>messenger of thy Lord</u>, that I may bestow on thee a holy son."

19:20 She said: "How shall I have a son, when man hath never touched me? and I am not unchaste."

19:21 He said: "So shall it be. Thy Lord hath said: 'Easy is this with me:' and we will make him a sign to mankind, and mercy from us. For it is a thing decreed."

19:22 And she conceived him, and retired with him to a far-off place. And the throes came upon her by the trunk of a palm. She said: "Oh, would that I had died ere this, and been a thing forgotten, forgotten quite!"

19:23 And one cried to her from below her: "Grieve not thou, thy Lord hath provided a streamlet at thy feet: –

19:24 And shake the trunk of the palm-tree toward thee: it will drop fresh ripe dates upon thee.

Sura 26

Sura 26 190-199 - The faithful spirit hath come down with this Book

26:190 In this was a sign, but most of them believed not.

26:191 But thy Lord! – He is the Mighty, the Mercilful!

26:192 Verily from the Lord of the Worlds hath this Book come down;

26:193 The <u>faithful spirit</u> hath come down with it

26:194 Upon thy heart, that thou mightest become a warner –

26:195 In the clear Arabic tongue:

26:196 And truly it is foretold in the Scriptures of them of yore.

26:197 Was it not a sign to them that the learned among the children of Israel recognised it?

26:198 If we had sent it down unto any foreigner,

26:199 And he had recited it to them, they had not believed.

Sura 98

Sura 98:1-3 - Gabriel implied as a messenger from God reciting the pure pages wherein are true Scriptures!

98:1 "The unbelievers among the people of the Book, and the Polytheisis, did not waver, until the CLEAR EVIDENCE had come to them,

98:2 A messenger from God, reciting to them the pure pages wherein are true Scriptures!

98:3 Neither were they to whom the Scriptures were given divided into sects, till after this clear evidence had reached them!"

MICHAEL

Sura 2

Sura 2:90-94 - Whoso is the enemy of Gabriel, angels, and Michael shall have God as his enemy

2:90 And thou wilt surely find them of all men most covetous of life, beyond even the polytheists. To be kept alive a thousand years might one of them desire: but that he may be preserved alive, shall no one reprieve himself from the punishment! And God seeth what they do.

2:91 Say: Whoso is the enemy of Gabriel – For he it is who by God's leave hath caused the Koran to descend on thy heart, the confirmation of previous revelations, and guidance, and good tidings to the faithful –

2:92 Whoso is an enemy to God or his <u>angels</u>, or to <u>Gabriel</u>, or to <u>Michael</u>, shall have God as his enemy: for verily God is an enemy to the Infidels.

2:93 Moreover, clear signs have we sent down to thee, and one will disbelieve them but the perverse.

2:94 Oft as they have formed an engagement with thee, will some of them set it aside? But most of them believe not.

ANGELS HARUT AND MARUT

Sura 2

Sura 2:95-100 - What was being taught was revealed to the two angels, Harut and Marut at Babel

2:95 And when there came to them an apostle from God, affirming the previous revelations made to them, some of those to whom the Scriptures were given, threw the Book of God behind their backs as if they knew it not:

2:96 And they followed what the Satans read in the reign of Solomon: not that Solomon was unbelieving, but the Satans were unbelieving.

2:97 Sorcery did they teach to men, and what had been revealed to the two <u>angels</u>, <u>Harut</u> and <u>Marut</u>, at Babel. Yet no man did these two teach until they had said "We are only a temptation. Be not then an unbeliever." From these two did men learn how to cause divisions between man and wife: but unless by leave of God, no man did they harm thereby. They learned, indeed, what would harm and not profit them; and yet they knew that he who bought that art should have no part in the life to come! And vile the price for which they have sold themselves, – if they had but known it!

2:98 But had they believed and feared God, better surely would have been the reward from God, – if they had but known it!

2:99 O you who believe! say not to our apostle, "Raina" (Look at us); but say, "Ondhorna" (Regard us). And attend to this; for, the Infidels shall suffer a grievous chastisement.

2:100 The unbelievers among the people of the Book, and among the dilators, desire not that any good should be sent down to you from your Lord: but God will shew His special mercy to whom He will, for He is of great bounty.

MESSENGERS

Sura 10

Sura 10:20-24 - Our messengers note down your plottings

10:20 Men were of one religion only: then they fell to variance: and had not a decree (of respite) previously gone forth from thy Lord, their differences had surely been decided between them!

10:21 They say: "Unless a sign be sent down to him from his Lord..." But Say: The hidden is only with God: wait therefore: I truly will be with you among those who wait.

10:22 And when after a trouble which had befallen them, we caused this people to taste of mercy, lo! a plot on their part against our signs! Say: Swifter to plot is God! Verily, our messengers note down your plottings.

10:23 He it is who enableth you to travel by land and sea, so that you go on He it is who enableth you to travel by land and sea, so that you go on board of ships – which sail on with them, with favouring breeze in which they rejoice. But if a tempestuous gale overtake them, and the billow come on them from every side, and they think that they are encompassed therewith, they call on God, professing sincere religion: – "Wouldst thou but rescue us from this, then will we indeed be of the thankful."

10:24 But when we have rescued them, lo! they commit unrighteous excesses on the earth! O men! assuredly your self-injuring excess is only an enjoyment of this life present: soon you return to us: and we will let you know what you have done!

Sura 11

Sura 11:80-84 - The Angels saying we are the messengers of thy Lord

11:80 And his people came rushing on towards him, for aforetime had they wrought this wickedness. He said, "O my people! these my daughters will be purer for you: fear God, and put me not to shame in my guests. Is there no rightminded man among you?"

11:81 They said, "Thou knowest now that we need not thy daughters; and thou well knowest what we require."

11:82 He said, "Would that I had strength to resist you, or that I could find refuge with some powerful chieftain."

11:83 The Angels said, "O Lot! verily, we are the messengers of thy Lord: they shall not touch tee: depart with thy family in the dead of night, and let not one of you turn back: as for thy wife, on her shall light what shall light on them. Verily, that with which they are threatened is for the morning. Is not the morning near?"

11:84 And when our decree came to be executed we turned those cities upside down, and we rained down upon them blocks of claystone one after another, marked by thy Lord himself. Nor are they far distant from the wicked Meccans.

Sura 22

Sura 22:70-76 - God chooseth messengers from among the angels

22:70 They worship beside God, that for which He hath sent down no warranty, and that of which they have no knowledge: but for those who commit this wrong, no helper!

22:71 And when our clear signs are rehearsed to them, thou mayst perceive disdain in the countenances of the Infidels. Scarce can they refrain from rushing to attack those who rehearse our signs to them!

22:72 Say: Shall I tell you of worse than this? The fire which God hath threatened to those who believer not! Wrteched the passage thither!

22:73 O men! a parable is set forth to you, wherefore hearken to it. Verily, they on whom you call beside God, cannot create a fly, though they assemble for it; and if the fly carry off aught from them, they cannot take it away from it! Weak the suppliant and the supplicated!

22:74 Unworthy the estimate they form of God! for God is right Powerful, Mighty!

22:75 God chooseth messengers from among the angels and from among men: verily, God Heareth, Seeth.

22:76 He knoweth what is before them and what is behind them; and unto God shall all things return.

Sura 29

Sura 29:30-34 - When our messengers came to Abraham and to Lot

29:30 And when our messengers came to Abraham with the tidings of a son, they said, "Of a truth we will destroy in in-dwellers in this city, for its in-dwellers are evil doers."

29:31 He said, "Lot is therein." They said, "We know full well who therein is.

29:32 Him and his family will we save, except his wife; she will be of those who linger.

29:33 And when our messengers came to Lot, he was troubled for them, and his arm was too weak to protect them; and they said, "Fear not, and distress not thyself, for thee and thy family will we save, except thy wife; she will be of those who linger.

29:34 We will surely bring down upon the dwellers in this city vengeance from Heaven for the excesses they have committed."

Acknowledgements

Thank you - Kay Stitzel and Sara Jess for your editing, organizing, and proofreading skills. Mike White, Publishing Consultant of Ghost River Images, for your talent in turning a manuscript into a beautiful book. And, of course, the Angels for your guidance, love, and constant encouragement.

About the Author

Kermie Wohlenhaus, Ph.D. is an author, TV producer, and angelologist. She teaches workshops and classes, gives angel presentations nationally, and hosts a TV show in Tucson, Arizona on public access called *Kermie & the Angels* which is available on YouTube.

As an angel expert, Dr. Wohlenhaus is regularly interviewed on TV, radio, podcasts, for newspapers and magazines throughout the United States. She is popular in live performances with radio and TV audiences for her knowledge and accurate angelic messages. Dr. Wohlenhaus is the Founder and Director of the School of Angel Studies.

Dr. Wohlenhaus has also authored *How to Talk and Actually Listen to Your Guardian Angel*, which is available in Spanish, French and German. *The Complete Reference to Angels in The Koran (Qur'an), The Complete Reference to Angels in the Bible, The Complete Reference to Angels in The Book of Mormon* and *The Complete Reference to Angels in Other Sacred Texts* are a series of references annotated by Dr. Wohlenhaus called *The Complete Reference to Angels in Sacred Texts*. These books are important foundation texts within the field of angelology, the study of angels.

Dr. Wohlenhaus received a Bachelor of Science (BS) from Colorado State University, a Master of Divinity (MDIV) from the Iliff School of Theology, and a Doctor of Philosophy (Ph.D.) in Religion/ Metaphysics at the College of Metaphysical Studies. She is currently living in Tucson, Arizona.

For further information: www.KermieandtheAngels.com

www.ingramcontent.com/pod-product-compliance
Lightning Source LLC
Chambersburg PA
CBHW071946100426
42736CB00042B/2284